an AMERICAN GIRL *in* LONDON

an AMERICAN GIRL *in* LONDON

120 Nourishing Recipes for Your Family from a Californian Expat

MARISSA HERMER

RODALE.

RODALE
wellness

Live happy. Be healthy. Get inspired.

Sign up today to get exclusive access to our authors, exclusive bonuses, and the most authoritative, useful, and cutting-edge information on health, wellness, fitness, and living your life to the fullest.

Visit us online at RodaleWellness.com

Join us at RodaleWellness.com/Join

© 2017 by Marissa Hermer

Rodale books may be purchased for business or promotional use or for special sales. For information, please write to:
Special Markets Department, Rodale Inc., 733 Third Avenue, New York, NY 10017

Printed in China

Rodale Inc. makes every effort to use acid-free ♾, recycled paper ♻.

Photographs by Helen Cathcart
Prop stylist: Linda Berlin
Food stylist & food writer: Dara Sutin
Assistant: Sophie Mackinnon
Book design by Rae Ann Spitzenberger

Library of Congress Cataloging-in-Publication Data is on file with the publisher.

ISBN 978–1–62336–815–9

Distributed to the trade by Macmillan

2   4   6   8   10   9   7   5   3   1
hardcover

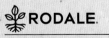

RODALE

We inspire health, healing, happiness, and love in the world. Starting with you.

Follow us @RodaleBooks on

to my family

---

*To my children, who make me feel like
the luckiest mummy in the world.*

*To my husband, for being my safety net
and my trampoline.*

contents

Introduction **ix**

introduction

WRITING THIS BOOK HAS BEEN A NEARLY IMPOSSIBLE TASK. I CLEARLY wasn't thinking at all. I just said, "Yes, I'll do it" (simultaneously believing I am invincible and can do anything—and also knowing that I'm not and I can't). I thought, "It can't be that hard to write a cookbook." Well, it is. It is really hard to write a book. It also doesn't help that I'm not a writer or a chef (and perhaps I drank the truth serum this morning!), but I am a home cook and wrote this during the kids' naptimes and on Saturday mornings when my husband took the munchkins to the park and when I've just forced myself to squeeze out any last focus that I have and write about food and family and love.

Growing up in Southern California, I was raised on avocados from my grandmother's tree. Our fish came from the fishermen on the docks in Newport Beach, and we picked the vegetables for our salads from the garden behind our house. I remember husking ears of corn on our patio in the summer and hauling huge watermelons from the dirt to the kitchen table for slippery seed-spitting contests. In autumn, our backyard was crawling with pumpkins—not the perfectly orange variety from the supermarket, but the warty, characterful kind—and the first sign of Christmas was when navel oranges popped up at our local farmers' market. My dad would bring a big red wagon to the citrus stalls and stock up on bags of oranges for juicing—and for my mother's Christmas morning mimosas.

I moved to New York City as an adult, and what I lost in locally grown produce and In-N-Out Burgers, I gained in experiencing a truly gastronomic-obsessed culture. Of course there are great restaurants in Orange County, but New York City is foodie-ism gone wild—and I dove right in. I became enchanted with Asian flavours, which I never had growing up in a beach town. I fell in love with American diner food and discovered dangerously addictive food trucks. With such a wide variety of quality ingredients and inspiring meals at my feet, cooking and eating became a daily adventure, and I was hooked.

When work took me to London 10 years ago, I packed my bags with a warning from my father ringing in my ears. He was sure I would hate England. "If I wanted my peas mushy, I would chew them myself," he said. Plus, there would be no avocados. Who could live with that?

He was wrong, of course. I loved Britain, with its warm pub culture and stellar Indian food, and to compound my appreciation of the UK, I met my husband-to-be shortly after moving (at a dinner party, of course). Matt is the restaurateur behind London's Bumpkin restaurants, and while seated next to him for the first time, I ordered from the vegetarian menu. He looked with disgust at my plate of zucchini and goat cheese tart. "Are you a vegetarian?" he asked in horror. "No, but sometimes I like eating meat-free," I replied. He couldn't understand this but let it pass, and we fell in love anyway. Clearly this man was a meat-and-potatoes Brit. I had my work cut out for me if I was ever going to cook for him.

Now, a decade, a British passport for my dual nationality, a marriage, and three children later, I still haven't found avocados that compare to those from my grandmother's tree. (Thankfully there are summers in Newport Beach, where I overdose on the green stuff, and it seems to carry me through the rest of the year.) A traditional Sunday roast has replaced my California Sunday beach BBQ, and British sticky toffee pudding has elbowed out the ultra-American s'mores. I learned how to cook the perfect roast potatoes for my potato-obsessed husband, and a great Irish stew to warm up the winter months. But as I made London my home, I also didn't want to lose my own Americana roots, and so I started incorporating little California twists into our family meals. We use sourdough bread for the traditional British Bread and Butter Pudding (giving it a sour-sweet flavour). I make loaded Sweet Potato Shepherd's Pie and our Bumpkin restaurant twist on eggs Benedict for when Matt wants a cooked breakfast: Eggs Montagu with cashew butter sauce and steamed spinach on a quinoa pancake. Our home kitchen may not delight traditionalists, but it's perfect for those who want to explore a culinary match made in transatlantic heaven. I've also taken huge delight in introducing my husband and our friends to some of my favourite Americana dishes from my childhood—Dad's Porridge, my godmother's Classic Apple Pie, and Zucchini Feta Muffins (or as I've learned to call them, corguettes).

As Matt and I have grown our family and expanded our restaurant business, I've had to think about my home cooking in a new way. Are my menus wholesome enough to grow my littles into bigs? Which recipes can I manage with my working mum schedule? And will my family actually eat the dishes I prepare? The front door is more of a revolving door of children for playdates and friends for supper, and my perspective in the kitchen has evolved to suit our lifestyle. I've discovered that a snack-stocked pantry is essential, and that children will eat anything if it is called a pancake (even quinoa!). I know that soups and smoothies are perfect for getting kiddies to eat vegetables, and that if I have muffins and breads made for breakfast, I can shove one in my breakfast-hating husband's hand for him to fuel the start of his day.

I've never thought of myself as a chef—I'm not one. I am a working mother who cooks easy recipes and keeps a growing family well fed. It is a balancing act, and one that I will never completely figure out. However, I do have a few tricks to keep my British husband happy, my picky children nourished, and my Californian soul satisfied.

morning to midday

PANCAKES

Every morning, my children—like all children who are awake—want pancakes. While I try to divert them with more inventive options, the truth is that they rarely say, "Mummy, I would like a Zucchini and Feta Muffin" or "Mummy, please can you make us Corn Fritters with Guacamole and Tomato Chutney?" It is all about the pancake. So in order to introduce some variety, I have a gold-standard pancake base that adapts easily. I often add sweet potato, bananas, rhubarb (hello pink pancakes), or pumpkin puree (Happy Halloween!) to mix things up and slip in different fruits and vegetables. If you are a parent, you understand when I say most mornings with children are like Groundhog Day. I can't help you talk your child out of the superman cape, but pancakes we have covered.

BASIC PANCAKES

This is the ultimate go-to pancake batter. Light and fluffy from the ricotta, the pancakes are simply irresistible with just a touch of sweetness from the honey and that crisp golden-brown edge. **MAKES 12**

2 cups all-purpose
  flour
1 teaspoon baking
  powder
Pinch salt
1 cup milk
1 cup fresh ricotta
  cheese
2 large eggs, gently
  beaten
1 tablespoon honey
½ teaspoon vanilla
  extract
¼ cup butter, melted
  and cooled, plus
  extra for cooking
Fresh fruit and maple
  syrup, to serve

1. In a large bowl, combine the flour, baking powder, and salt. Form a well in the centre and pour in the milk, ricotta cheese, and eggs. Gently whisk together, then add the honey, vanilla, and butter, continuing to whisk until a smooth batter is formed. Allow the batter to rest for 10 minutes.

2. In a large frying pan over medium heat, add a knob of butter, swirling the pan to coat. Add 2 to 3 tablespoons of the batter to the pan. When bubbles begin to form at the surface, about 2 to 3 minutes, turn the pancake and cook for another 1 to 2 minutes. Repeat.

3. Serve the pancakes warm, topped with fresh fruit and a drizzle of maple syrup.

TIPS: *I premix the dry ingredients of my basic pancake recipe and keep a container in the pantry. When I'm ready to cook, I add the milk, eggs, cheese, butter, and any other mix-ins. The simple preparation keeps things moving quickly during time-scarce mornings.*

I like to keep the pancakes warm in a low oven while I make batches—just place them on a lined baking tray at 80°F (or your lowest oven setting) until you've finished cooking.

BUCKWHEAT PANCAKES WITH BLUEBERRIES

Wholesome and nutty, buckwheat flour is a great alternative for those trying to cut back on processed flours or for anyone who has an intolerance to gluten. They are not only gluten-free but dairy-free as well. It's best to make these pancakes slightly smaller as the lack of gluten, which is a binding agent, makes them more delicate to flip.

MAKES 8–10

½ cup buckwheat flour

½ cup brown rice flour

1 teaspoon baking powder

1 teaspoon baking soda

Pinch of salt

2 tablespoons honey

1 teaspoon ground cinnamon

1 cup almond milk

¼ cup coconut milk yoghurt

1 large egg

½ teaspoon vanilla extract

2 tablespoons coconut oil

½ cup wild blueberries

Honey or maple syrup, to serve

1. In a large mixing bowl, combine the buckwheat flour, brown rice flour, baking powder, baking soda, and salt.

2. In a large bowl, whisk together the honey, cinnamon, almond milk, yoghurt, egg, and vanilla. Gradually pour into the dry ingredients, whisking to combine. The batter should be slightly lumpy.

3. Heat a large frying pan over medium-low heat, add a knob of coconut oil, and swirl to coat the pan. Spoon a couple of tablespoons of the batter into the pan. Cook for 2 to 3 minutes, or until bubbles begin to form on the surface. Sprinkle with blueberries, then turn and cook for another 1 to 2 minutes, or until golden brown.

4. Serve warm with a drizzle of honey or maple syrup.

SWEET POTATO PANCAKES

These pancakes require a bit more prep time, but the delicious, warming flavour of the sweet potato is worth it. They are a good source of vitamins A and C and incredibly kid friendly. **MAKES 30**

1 cup mashed sweet potato (2 sweet potatoes)

2 cups milk

1 cup plain yoghurt

2 large eggs, lightly beaten

¼ cup butter, melted and cooled, plus extra for cooking

2½ cups all-purpose flour

1 teaspoon baking powder

½ teaspoon baking soda

1 teaspoon ground cinnamon

½ teaspoon ground nutmeg

Pinch of salt

Maple syrup, to serve

Chopped nuts such as walnuts or pecans, to serve

1. In a large bowl, whisk together the sweet potato, milk, yoghurt, eggs, and cooled butter until smooth.

2. In a separate bowl, whisk together the flour, baking powder, baking soda, cinnamon, nutmeg, and salt. Add the wet ingredients gradually to the dry, whisking together. Allow the batter to rest for 10 minutes.

3. Heat a large frying pan over medium heat. Add a knob of butter and swirl to coat the pan. Add a couple heaping tablespoons of the batter and cook for 2 to 3 minutes, or until bubbles begin to form at the surface. Turn and cook for another 1 to 2 minutes, or until golden.

4. Serve warm with a drizzle of maple syrup and a sprinkling of chopped nuts.

TIP: *I keep roasted or boiled pieces of sweet potato ready to go in my refrigerator or freezer, making it easy to add some goodness into soups, salads, and of course these pancakes!*

ZUCCHINI FETA MUFFINS
(UK TRANSLATION: COURGETTE FETA MUFFINS)

We are more of a muffin family than a loaf family, though this recipe makes a wonderful, more traditional zucchini loaf with a slightly cooler oven temperature (about 325°F) and longer cooking time. Our preference comes down to simplicity because it is easier to grab-and-go with a muffin. My family loves these savoury muffins in the morning, but they are also great for after-school snacks. **MAKES 12**

1 cup grated zucchini (1 medium)

1 cup grated carrot

2 tablespoons olive oil

2 spring onions, finely sliced

¾ cup whole milk

2 large eggs, lightly beaten

1 cup whole meal flour

1 cup all-purpose flour

1 teaspoon baking powder

½ teaspoon baking soda

2 teaspoons chile flakes

2 teaspoons ground cumin

1 teaspoon salt

¼ cup coriander, finely chopped

¼ cup toasted pumpkin seeds

½ cup crumbled feta cheese

¼ cup raisins or sultanas

1. Preheat the oven to 350°F. Line a 12-mould muffin tray with paper cups.

2. In a large bowl, whisk together the zucchini, carrot, olive oil, onions, milk, and eggs.

3. In a separate bowl, whisk together the flour, baking powder, baking soda, chile flakes, cumin, and salt. Gradually add the wet ingredients to the dry, stirring to combine. Stir through the coriander, pumpkin seeds, feta, and raisins.

4. Divide the batter among the individual cups and bake for 25 minutes, or until puffed and golden brown. Allow to cool before serving with a lashing of butter.

TIPS: *I like to use an ice cream scoop to get the perfect measure of batter into the moulds every time. Make a batch the night before and reheat them for breakfast.*

BLUEBERRY CHIA MUFFINS

These muffins are a great grab-and-go healthy breakfast option. Low in sugar but packed with flavour, they also happen to be vegan. Best kept 4 to 5 days in an airtight container. **MAKES 12**

2 cups rolled oats

2 tablespoons chia seeds

6 tablespoons water

1 cup mashed banana (approximately 3 medium-size bananas)

¼ cup maple syrup

¼ cup coconut oil, melted

¼ cup coconut yoghurt

1 teaspoon vanilla extract

2 teaspoons ground cinnamon

1 teaspoon ground ginger

1 teaspoon ground cardamom

1 teaspoon baking powder

½ teaspoon baking soda

¼ teaspoon salt

½ cup frozen or fresh blueberries

Crumble

1 tablespoon finely chopped walnuts

¼ cup oats

1 tablespoon maple syrup

1 tablespoon coconut oil

1. Preheat the oven to 375°F and line a 12-muffin tin with paper cases.

2. Place 1½ cups of the oats in a food processor and blend until a flour has formed. Stir through the remaining oats.

3. Add the chia seeds to the water and soak for 5 minutes. In a large bowl, whisk together the chia mixture, banana, maple syrup, coconut oil, coconut yoghurt, and vanilla. Add the oats, cinnamon, ginger, cardamom, baking powder, baking soda, and salt, and stir until a slightly lumpy batter has formed. Stir through the blueberries.

4. In a small bowl, mix together the walnuts, oats, maple syrup, and coconut oil.

5. Divide the batter into the individual cases and sprinkle the crumble over the top of each. Bake for 25 minutes, or until golden brown.

TIP: *An easy substitute for eggs in vegan baking is called a chia egg. By soaking the chia seeds in water for about 5 minutes, they bloom and have the same protein properties as an egg when baked.*

BANANA DATE MUFFINS

These muffins, which are sweet and rich but not too indulgent, are the perfect morning pick-me-up or late afternoon snack. Muffins freeze brilliantly, so I like to make double batches and then defrost them as needed. They are particularly useful when my husband forgets to eat breakfast and I can shove one in his hand as he walks out the door. **MAKES 12**

3 ripe bananas
⅓ cup butter, softened
½ cup brown sugar
¼ cup granulated sugar
2 eggs, lightly beaten
½ teaspoon vanilla extract
½ teaspoon ground cinnamon
½ cup rolled oats
1 cup all-purpose flour
1 teaspoon baking soda
½ teaspoon baking powder
¼ teaspoon salt
¼ cup milk of your choice (I like to use buttermilk)
½ cup roughly chopped Medjool dates
½ cup chopped nuts or pecan pieces
1 tablespoon demerara sugar

1. Preheat the oven to 350°F. Line a 12-muffin tin with paper cases.

2. In a small bowl, mash the bananas with a fork until smooth and set aside. In a separate bowl, using an electric hand whisk, whisk the butter with both sugars until pale and fluffy, about 3 minutes. Gradually add the eggs, whisking to combine. Add the vanilla and cinnamon. Stir through the mashed bananas.

3. In a small food processor, blitz the rolled oats to a fine crumb. Tip into a bowl and add the flour, baking soda, baking powder, and salt, stirring to combine. Gently fold the flour mixture into the wet ingredients, alternating with the milk. Be careful not to overmix. Stir through the chopped dates and ¼ cup of the chopped nuts.

4. Using an ice cream scoop, fill the muffin tray up to the top of each paper cup, and sprinkle with the remaining nuts and the sugar. Bake for 22 minutes, or until golden and puffed up. Serve warm with lashings of butter.

TIPS: *Oat flour adds a nice texture and some fiber. You can easily substitute frozen berries or toasted nuts for the dates.*

Turn this mix into the ultimate banana bread. Simply spoon the batter into a 9-inch x 5-inch loaf pan lined with parchment paper and bake at 350°F for 45 to 50 minutes, or until golden and a wooden pick comes out clean.

I like to use an ice cream scoop to get a perfect measure every time.

MOM'S GRANOLA

I was born in Laguna Beach, home of Birkenstocks and beach-loving hippies. Though my parents were never the "love-in" types, they were and will always be interested in a wholesome approach to food. So while my husband was raised on Marmite and toast, I was weaned on my mom's granola. Granola for breakfast (with milk or yoghurt), granola (made into granola bars) for an after-school snack, and granola for dessert (with a bit of ice cream). Every Christmas my mom would quadruple her monthly granola batch, and I remember spooning it into Kilner jars and wrapping big red ribbons around them . . . Christmas presents sorted!

Over the years, I've adapted the original recipe many times. Though I'm not gluten-free, gluten-free oats are easy to find, and I don't feel like I'm missing out, so I occasionally swap them for the regular variety. I also suffer from hay fever and have always been told that a spoonful of manuka honey helps to combat the seasonal wave of symptoms, so if I'm battling allergies, I'll throw in some of that, too. I add a lot of nuts and seeds to my batches because these give me protein to get me through the morning school run and on to work, though the exact ingredients fluctuate based on what I have in the cupboard. Though I now live very far from California, a bowl of granola makes me feel at home wherever I am. **SERVES 16**

2 cups large flaked oats

1 cup buckwheat groats

½ cup roughly chopped walnuts

¼ cup slivered almonds

½ cup flaked coconut

¼ cup pumpkin seeds

¼ cup sunflower seeds

1 tablespoon sesame seeds

¼ cup coconut oil

3 Medjool dates, roughly chopped

1 tablespoon ground cinnamon

½ cup maple syrup

2 tablespoons water

1. Preheat the oven to 300°F. Line a large baking tray with parchment paper and set aside.

2. In a large bowl, combine the oats, groats, walnuts, almonds, coconut, and seeds, stirring to combine.

3. Set a small saucepan over medium heat. Add the coconut oil, dates, cinnamon, maple syrup, and water. Gently bring to a boil, then reduce the heat to a simmer and cook for 3 minutes, or until the dates have softened. Transfer to a food processor and process until smooth.

4. Pour the date mixture onto the oat mixture and use a spatula to stir until thoroughly combined. This may take a couple of minutes.

recipe continues

5. Spread the mixture onto the lined baking tray and bake for 50 minutes, stirring halfway through. Allow to cool completely before placing into an airtight container.

TIPS: *Naturally sweetened with dates and maple syrup, this granola is great served with warm almond milk, on top of yoghurt, or, better yet, made into the perfect granola bar.*

If you want to cut down on the sugar, remove the dates from the recipe. Whisk 1 large egg white until stiff peaks form and fold through the mixture after you've added the hot liquid.

MOM'S GRANOLA BARS

To turn this delicious granola into bars, follow the directions above, adding ¾ cup almond (or other preferred nut) butter to the mixture over the stove in step 3. Stir through the oat-nut mixture, and transfer to a greased 8-inch x 8-inch baking dish. Flatten the mixture into the dish, and bake for 1 hour, until set and golden on top. Allow to cool a little, then slice into 16 bars and store in an airtight container. Melt 1.7 ounces of dark chocolate to drizzle over the bars for extra oomph! **MAKES 16**

DAD'S PORRIDGE

In my childhood home, my mother did most of the cooking, but my father had a few special dishes. During wet winter mornings, he would invariably be at the stove preparing our morning porridge.

I remember watching him add handfuls of raisins and chopped apples to the pot, sweetening the boiling water before adding the oats. I now make my family's porridge the same way. Ahead of busy days, I even like to make an enormous batch on a Monday and pour the finished mixture into a loaf pan. Once it has cooled to room temperature, I pop the pan into the refrigerator, and for the rest of the week, I cut slices of the porridge loaf and simply heat them up for breakfast. It couldn't be faster or easier, and the scent on a cold morning is hugely comforting. **SERVES 4 TO 6**

1½ cups milk
1½ cups water
Pinch of salt
1 apple, chopped
½ cup raisins
2 cups organic gluten-free porridge oats
Handful of seeds (chia seeds, flaxseeds, sunflower seeds, and pumpkin seeds work well)
1 cup milk, to serve
½ tablespoon Greek yoghurt, to serve
2 tablespoons honey, to serve

1. In a saucepan, combine the milk, water, and salt over high heat. Add the apple and raisins, bring to a boil, and simmer for 2 to 3 minutes. Add the oats, stirring to combine. Reduce the heat, simmering gently for 4 minutes. Stir slowly until the oats reach a nice consistency. Add more milk if you prefer to have the oats a bit softer. Leave to stand for 2 minutes before eating.

2. To serve, pour into bowls, topping each serving with some of the milk, yoghurt, a sprinkling of the seeds, or honey.

TIP: *To make a batch ahead of time for a busy week, skip the milk in the beginning (as it will stay in the fridge longer) and just use 4 cups water, 2½ cups of oats, ¾ cup raisins, and 1 to 2 apples. While the mixture is still warm and before it sets, pour it into a loaf pan for easy slicing throughout the week. Then simply slice off what you want for breakfast the next day, pop it in the microwave, and add the milk when you are ready to eat.*

I sometimes add a pinch of cinnamon and/or nutmeg to the pot or on top of my bowl.

CORN FRITTERS

This is one of my favourite breakfasts. My children wake up and want pancakes, my husband wakes up and wants coffee, and I wake up and want guacamole (you can take the girl out of California, but you can't take the California out of the girl!). After making corn pancakes for my kids, I experimented with the recipe and ended up with these corn fritters, which are the perfect vehicle for shoveling avocado into my mouth. If I'm feeling particularly festive—or have friends coming over for brunch—I add my Tomato Chutney (page 221) on top, which is delicious and looks impressive. **SERVES 4**

¾ cup all-purpose flour

½ teaspoon baking powder

1 teaspoon ground cumin

1 teaspoon smoked paprika

1 teaspoon salt

1 large egg, lightly beaten

Zest and juice from 1 lime

½ cup water

1 cup tinned corn, drained

½ red onion, finely chopped

1 green chili pepper, finely chopped

2 tablespoons finely chopped coriander

2 tablespoons olive oil

Guacamole

2 avocados, lightly mashed

½ teaspoon chili flakes

1 lime, juiced

2 tablespoons fresh coriander, to garnish

1. In a large bowl, combine the flour, baking powder, cumin, paprika, and salt. Make a well in the centre and add the egg, lime juice and zest, and water, stirring to combine. Fold through the sweet corn, onion, chili, and coriander.

2. Heat a large nonstick frying pan over medium heat. Add 1 tablespoon of the olive oil and drop a couple of tablespoons of batter into the pan. Allow bubbles to come to the surface before turning over. You will need to do this in batches with the remaining olive oil.

3. *To make the guacamole:* In a small bowl, combine the avocados, chili flakes, lime juice, and a pinch of salt, mashing gently.

4. Place 2 fritters on a plate and garnish with a dollop of avocado mash and fresh coriander. Serve with Tomato Chutney (page 221).

TIPS: *You can top the fritters with plain avocado if you are pressed for time. I also love serving with my PFG (Pea-Feta Guacamole, page 154), for a morning feast. You can make the fritters ahead of time and keep them warm in the oven on low heat until you're ready to serve them. Make them even more decadent by topping them with olive oil–fried eggs and some crumbled feta cheese or add a dollop of sour cream.*

SMOOTHIES

I'm a smoothie girl. I usually end up throwing one of my morning concoctions into my son's Batman thermos en route to a morning meeting or spooning it out of a mug at my desk. I love a smoothie because not only is it mostly hands-free eating (okay, spooning it into your mouth takes one hand), but I also get to be creative first thing in the morning as my smoothie is different every time. The contents depend on (1) what is in my fridge and (2) what I'm feeling. I enjoy scooping in different superfoods and superseeds when I feel I'm in need of a bit more of this or a bit more of that.

SERVES 1–2

Toss all ingredients into a blender and mix until well blended.

Favourite Toppings

HEMP SEEDS: A complete, plant-based source of protein and high in fiber, hemp seeds add a nice crunch and a nutty taste.

BEE POLLEN: You need only 1 teaspoon a day of this incredible nutrient- and mineral-rich whole food. It lends a gorgeous honey flavour and beautiful colour.

CHIA SEEDS: Not only do they keep hunger at bay, they are a complete protein and high in omega-3 fats.

GREEN GODDESS SMOOTHIE

1 frozen banana
½ avocado
Small handful of spinach (or kale)
½ lemon, juiced
1 Medjool date, pitted
1 tablespoon nut butter
1 cup coconut water

CHOCOLATE PEANUT BUTTER SHAKE

1 frozen banana
2 tablespoons cacao powder
1 tablespoon peanut butter
1 tablespoon maple syrup
1 cup almond milk

recipe continues

TIP: *Frozen bananas are a great trick for making a creamy smoothie. I like to freeze my peeled bananas in a resealable plastic bag so they are ready to go when I need one in a pinch.*

BLUEBERRY COCONUT CASHEW SMOOTHIE

½ **avocado**
½ **cup frozen blueberries**
1½ **teaspoons honey**
½ **teaspoon vanilla extract**
1 **tablespoon cashew butter**
1½ **cups coconut milk**

EGGS MONTAGU ON QUINOA PANCAKES WITH CASHEW CREAM

I love Eggs Benedict—it reminds me of my 20s in Manhattan when brunch meant a round of Bloody Marys—but I'm not 20 anymore and neither is my metabolism. Enter Julie Montagu, whom I met while filming *Ladies of London*. Thankfully, she introduced me to her version of my Eggs Benedict, which is healthy and filling but absolutely delicious. It doesn't weigh me down and reminds me of the good old days without the food hangover! **SERVES 2 (4 TO 6 PATTIES)**

½ cup white beans, rinsed and drained

1 egg

2 egg whites

1 green onion, finely chopped

1 teaspoon ground cumin

1 cup grated Cheddar

1½ cups cooked quinoa

⅓ cup self-rising flour

Salt, to taste

Ground black pepper, to taste

1–2 tablespoons light olive oil

1 tablespoon vinegar

4 eggs

2 large handfuls baby spinach

1 avocado, sliced

2 green onions, thinly sliced, to garnish

1 tablespoon fresh coriander leaves, to garnish

Cashew Cream (page 24), to serve

1. In a food processor, combine the beans, egg, egg whites, green onion, cumin, and cheese. Pulse until combined. Tip into a large bowl and mix in the quinoa and flour. Season with salt and pepper. Form into 4 patties and then place in the refrigerator to firm up for at least 10 minutes.

2. In a large frying pan over medium heat, heat the olive oil. Cook the patties for 8 to 10 minutes on each side, or until crisp and golden.

3. Place a medium pot of water on the stove and bring to a boil. Add the vinegar and reduce the heat to a simmer. Stir the water rapidly to create a vortex, then crack an egg into the centre. Wait for 30 seconds before dropping the next egg in. Cook the eggs for 3 to 5 minutes, then repeat with the remaining 2 eggs.

4. Serve the cakes topped with the spinach and poached eggs, along with a side of avocado and garnishes of green onions and coriander, and a good dollop of Cashew Cream.

TIP: *Make extra quinoa pancakes—I love these topped with Hummus (page 158) as an afternoon snack!*

recipe continues

CASHEW CREAM

1⅓ cups cashews,
    soaked in water
    for at least 2 hours
1 clove garlic
2 tablespoons lime
    or lemon juice
½ teaspoon salt
1–1½ cups water

Drain and rinse the soaked cashews. Tip into a high-speed blender along with the garlic, lemon or lime juice, salt, and water and blend until smooth. Add more or less water depending on desired consistency.

TIPS: *Cashew cream is a great alternative as a dairy-free condiment. You need only a small amount because it's quite rich, and it will keep well in the fridge for 3 to 5 days. Stir before using and dilute with water if it becomes too thick.*

Pimp your cashew cream by adding fresh herbs like basil or mint to the mix.

KITCHEN SINK FRITTATAS

I could write an "Ode to Frittata," there are so many reasons why I love them: They can be served hot or cold; they are easier to make than quiche (no pastry); they are healthier than a quiche (no pastry); they are a great way to use up leftovers; they can be a breakfast, lunch, or dinner; they are protein packed; they can be made in muffin tins for individual portions (and are also easy to freeze) or in a big skillet to serve a crowd; and they can be made ahead of time (moms, get excited!). Basically, they are the perfect food. I love sneaking in veggies such as spinach or broccoli for the kids and I'll sometimes add cheese or sun-dried tomatoes, or whatever else needs to be used up in my fridge. Truly, everything but the kitchen sink. **SERVES 6**

PANCETTA, ONION, AND CHIVE FRITTATA

8 small, waxy potatoes, cubed

¼ cup olive oil

2 sweet white onions such as Vidalia, thinly sliced

2 cloves garlic, minced

½ cup diced pancetta or bacon

Salt, to taste

Ground black pepper, to taste

8 large eggs

¼ cup heavy cream

1 tablespoon balsamic vinegar

1 cup grated Parmesan cheese

¼ cup finely chopped chives, plus extra for garnish

1. Preheat the broiler to the maximum setting.

2. Bring a pot of water to a boil over medium heat. Add the potatoes and cook for 8 to 10 minutes, or until tender. Drain.

3. Place a large, ovenproof skillet over medium heat. Add the olive oil and onions. Cook for 20 minutes, or until golden and caramelized, stirring every so often. Add the garlic and pancetta and cook for 6 to 8 minutes, or until beginning to brown. Stir through the cooked potatoes and season the mixture well with salt and black pepper.

4. In a bowl, whisk together the eggs, cream, vinegar, cheese, and chives. Pour the mix into the frying pan. Cover and cook over low-medium heat until the edges are brown and the mixture is almost set, about 10 to 15 minutes. Remove the cover and place the entire thing underneath the broiler for 5 minutes, or until the mixture has fully set and the top is turning a golden brown. Garnish with chives and serve.

MUSHROOM, LEEK, AND THYME FRITTATA

¼ cup olive oil

2 medium leeks, cleaned, halved, and thinly sliced

2 cloves garlic, minced

1½ cups mixed mushrooms, cleaned and roughly chopped (I like to use cremini, button, and portobello)

2 tablespoons finely chopped fresh thyme

Salt, to taste

Ground black pepper, to taste

8 large eggs

½ cup heavy cream

¼ cup grated Pecorino cheese

½ cup grated Fontina cheese

1. Preheat the broiler to the maximum setting.

2. Place a large, ovenproof skillet over medium heat. Add the olive oil and leeks and cook for 10 to 12 minutes, or until the leeks are soft and translucent. Add the garlic and sauté for another 2 minutes. Increase the heat to high and add the mushrooms. Cook for 6 to 8 minutes, or until any water has evaporated and the mushrooms are soft. Sprinkle over the thyme and season well with salt and black pepper.

3. In a bowl, whisk together the eggs, cream, Pecorino cheese, and Fontina cheese. Pour the mix into the frying pan. Cover and cook over medium-low heat until the edges are brown and the mixture is almost set, 10 to 12 minutes. Remove the cover and place the entire thing underneath the broiler for 5 minutes, or until the mixture has fully set and the top is turning a golden brown.

KALE, TOMATO, AND FETA FRITTATA

¼ cup olive oil

1 sweet potato, peeled and cubed

1 small red onion, finely chopped

2 cloves garlic, minced

2 cups kale, stems removed and leaves roughly chopped

1 pint cherry tomatoes, halved

½ cup pitted kalamata olives, roughly chopped

8 large eggs

2 tablespoons shredded fresh basil

1 tablespoon chopped fresh oregano

Salt, to taste

Ground black pepper, to taste

1 cup crumbled feta cheese

1. Preheat the broiler to the maximum setting.

2. Place a large, ovenproof skillet over medium heat. Add the olive oil and sweet potato. Cook for 10 to 15 minutes, or until fork-tender. Add the onion and garlic and sauté for 8 minutes, or until soft and translucent.

3. Add the kale and cook for 5 minutes, or until wilted. Add the cherry tomatoes and olives and cook another 5 minutes.

4. Meanwhile, whisk together the eggs, basil, and oregano. Season well with salt and black pepper. Stir through the feta cheese gently. Pour the mix over the vegetables in the frying pan. Cover and cook over low-medium heat until the edges are brown and the mixture is almost set, 10 to 12 minutes. Remove the cover and place the entire thing underneath the broiler for 5 minutes, or until the mixture has fully set and the top is turning a golden brown.

TIP: *I like my frittatas to have little bit of bulk to them, so I often include potatoes or squash, but you could easily omit.*

TRADITIONAL ENGLISH BREAKFAST

The traditional English Breakfast (aka fry-up) is big in Britain. During Georgian and Victorian times, breakfast was an integral part of any English shooting weekend or hunt because it was an opportunity to show off the ingredients (like bacon, sausages, and eggs) that were produced on the estate. Breakfast was the time to brag. Later during the Industrial Revolution, the full English Breakfast was enjoyed by the working classes as a hearty meal first thing in the morning, which kept physical labourers full throughout the day. Now walking around London, the traditional fry-up is served in street cafés and also in luxury hotels—and, of course, in my own kitchen on the weekends with a newspaper and a pot of hot coffee while the munchkins nap. Here, I've elevated the standard English Breakfast to pack in more flavour and freshness. **SERVES 4**

Baked Beans
1 tablespoon olive oil
½ red onion, finely chopped
½ cup diced pancetta or bacon
1 clove garlic, minced
1 can (8 ounces) chopped tomatoes
1 tablespoon brown sugar
1 tablespoon cider vinegar
1 can (14 ounces) white beans, such as cannellini, drained and rinsed
1–2 sprigs fresh thyme
Salt and ground black pepper, to taste

1. *To make the beans:* Heat the oil in a large skillet over medium heat. Add the onion and pancetta and cook for 6 to 8 minutes, stirring, until golden brown.

2. Stir in the garlic, tomatoes, brown sugar, vinegar, and 1 cup water. Stir through the beans and thyme. Bring to a boil, reduce the heat, and cook for 1 hour, stirring occasionally, until you have a thick sauce.

3. Season with salt and black pepper. This can be made up to 3 days in advance and stored in the fridge in an airtight container.

recipe continues

Sautéed Mushrooms
1 tablespoon olive oil
2 cups mixed mushrooms, cleaned and roughly chopped (such as button, portobellini)
1 clove garlic, minced
Salt and ground black pepper, to taste

8 slices bacon
4 breakfast sausages
2 tablespoons olive oil, divided
8 eggs
6–8 slices thick sourdough bread

4. *To make the mushrooms:* Heat the oil in a large skillet over high heat. Add the mushrooms and cook for 6 to 8 minutes, or until all of the water has evaporated and they are soft and beginning to turn golden. Add the garlic halfway through the cooking time. Season well with salt and pepper.

5. Preheat the oven to 400°F. Line a baking tray with parchment paper. Arrange the bacon and sausages and drizzle with 1 tablespoon of olive oil. Bake for 10 minutes, or until golden.

6. Meanwhile, heat the remaining 1 tablespoon olive oil in a pan and fry the eggs for 5 to 7 minutes, or until the whites have set and the yolks are warm.

7. To serve, arrange 2 slices of bacon, 1 sausage, 2 fried eggs, a generous scoop of baked beans, and mushrooms on the plate. Serve with sourdough toast.

HEALTHIER ENGLISH BREAKFAST

This is an equally delicious and satisfying breakfast, packed with healthy omega fats from the avocado and iron from the dark leafy greens. I like to poach the eggs instead of frying, which requires a bit more attention but cuts down on oil. Serve alongside the baked beans and sautéed mushrooms. **SERVES 4**

1 teaspoon vinegar

4 eggs

2 tablespoons olive oil, divided

1 clove garlic, minced

1 teaspoon chili flakes

2 cups roughly chopped cavolo nero or kale, stems removed

Juice from ½ lemon

Salt and ground black pepper, to taste

8 slices Halloumi cheese

2 avocados, halved, pitted, and thinly sliced

Baked Beans (page 30)

Sautéed Mushrooms (opposite)

1. Place a medium pot of water on the stove and bring to a boil. Add the vinegar and reduce the heat to a simmer. Stir the water rapidly to create a vortex, then crack an egg in the centre. Wait for 30 seconds before dropping the next egg in. Cook the eggs for 3 to 5 minutes, then repeat with the remaining eggs.

2. Heat 1 tablespoon oil in a large skillet over medium heat. Add the garlic and chili flakes and cook for 1 to 2 minutes, or until fragrant. Add the greens and cook for 4 to 6 minutes, or until wilted. Remove from the heat and stir through the lemon juice. Season with salt and black pepper.

3. Place the pan back on the heat. Add the remaining 1 tablespoon of oil and sauté the Halloumi slices. Cook for 2 to 3 minutes per side, or until golden and crisp.

4. Divide the greens among the plates and top with 2 slices of cheese and the poached eggs. Serve alongside slices of avocado with good helpings of beans and mushrooms on the plate. Give yourself a pat on the back for being so healthy! Now you deserve some Sticky Toffee Pudding (page 202).

TOAST SOLDIERS
(AKA EGGS GRANDMA)

I grew up eating Eggs Grandma, which is just the name of the eggs my grandmother used to cook. She would soft boil the eggs and toast the bread, and then chop everything and mix it all up in a little bowl for me to eat. When I moved to England, I discovered toast soldiers, which is essentially the same thing my grandma made, except a bit more presentable than the runny mess I grew up on. My kids love toast soldiers, or rather, they love the egg cups that come with the soft-boiled eggs. We have quite a collection now, and they always add some fun to our breakfast table. **SERVES 2**

4 eggs

4 slices sourdough bread

1 tablespoon butter, softened

1 tablespoon Marmite spread

Salt and ground black pepper, to taste

1. Bring a large pot of water to a boil. Gently lower the eggs into the pot, then swirl the water carefully with a spoon. Cook for 5 minutes.

2. Meanwhile, toast the bread, spread with butter and Marmite, then cut each piece of bread into thin strips.

3. When the eggs are ready, carefully remove them with a slotted spoon and place them in egg cups. Tap the top of each egg gently with a spoon and remove the top. Sprinkle with salt and pepper and dip in!

JAZZED-UP SOLDIERS

If you want to jazz up your soldiers, top them with a Dijon cheese mixture.

4 slices sourdough bread

¼ cup unsalted butter, melted

1 teaspoon smooth Dijon mustard

⅓ cup finely grated Gruyère cheese

2 tablespoons finely grated Romano cheese

1 tablespoon finely chopped parsley

1 tablespoon finely chopped thyme

Salt and ground black pepper, to taste

1. Preheat the oven to 400°F. Place the bread slices (sliced in 4 strips) in a shallow, wide dish.

2. Whisk together the butter and mustard and pour over the bread slices.

3. Sprinkle with the cheeses, parsley, and thyme. Add salt and pepper to taste.

4. Scatter the bread on a baking tray and bake for 20 minutes, or until golden.

BAKED BROWN BUTTER FRENCH TOAST

I'll never forget the first time I made French toast for the kids. The kiddies were delighted with their new favourite breakfast, and I felt quite clever for adding another menu item to our morning repertoire. It was such a hit that they were singing songs about the French toast. Declarations of love were made. And then my husband came into the kitchen—"Oh! You guys are eating *eggy bread!*" And with that, another Anglo-American debate ensued about who was right—is it Mommy, who calls it French toast, or Daddy, who calls it eggy bread (which is what it is called in England). Daddy always wins, of course—the benefit of having the home field advantage. The good news is that it tastes the same, whatever you call it. And you can put it together the night before, making your Sunday morning brunch routine that much easier. **SERVES A CROWD (10 TO 12)**

¼ **cup butter, plus extra for greasing**

16–18 **slices enriched bread such as challah or brioche, halved**

1 **pint blueberries**

6 **large eggs, lightly beaten**

2 **cups whole milk or buttermilk**

1 **cup heavy cream**

1 **tablespoon ground cinnamon**

1 **tablespoon honey or maple syrup**

1 **teaspoon vanilla extract**

1 **tablespoon demerara sugar**

Plain yoghurt, to serve

Maple syrup, to serve

1. In a small frying pan over medium heat, melt the butter. Swirl the pan and cook for 3 to 5 minutes, or until it turns a rich golden colour. Remove from the heat and set aside.

2. Generously butter a 9-inch x 9-inch baking dish. Using a pastry brush, paint the slices of bread with the browned butter. Lay the slices, slightly overlapping, into the baking dish along with a sprinkling of the blueberries.

3. In a bowl, whisk the eggs, milk, cream, cinnamon, honey or maple syrup, and vanilla together, then pour over the bread. Cover and refrigerate overnight.

4. Preheat the oven to 375°F. Sprinkle the demerara sugar over the entire dish and bake for 25 minutes, or until puffed up and golden. Serve warm with dollops of yoghurt and maple syrup.

TIP: *You can add any fruits you like, fresh or dried, to the mix. Some of my favourite combinations are dark chocolate and banana or cinnamon-coated apples.*

KEDGEREE

We often have friends over for weekend breakfasts, so I'm always looking for new, quick dishes to feed a crowd. When I stumbled across kedgeree, I added it to my weekend routine. Kedgeree is traditionally served with soft-boiled eggs, but we are a family of fried egg lovers, so it's fried for us. I love the Indian flavours—which are usually reserved for Friday nights in with a curry—being incorporated into breakfast.

The name *kedgeree* is thought to have originated with *khichri,* an Indian rice-and-bean dish that was brought back by British colonials who introduced it as a breakfast dish in the Victorian period. **SERVES 6**

2 cups milk
2 bay leaves
1 tablespoon black peppercorns
2½ cups smoked haddock, skinned
2 tablespoons vegetable oil
1 onion, minced
1 clove garlic, minced
1 tablespoon curry powder
1 teaspoon ground coriander
1 teaspoon ground turmeric
Pinch of cayenne pepper, to taste
3 cups cooked rice
½ cup roughly chopped coriander, plus extra for garnish
½ cup roughly chopped parsley, plus extra for garnish
Salt and black pepper
1 cup plain yoghurt
1 lime, juice and zest
1 tablespoon olive oil
6 eggs

1. In a medium pot, combine the milk, bay leaves, and peppercorns. Bring to a simmer, reduce the heat to low, add the fish, and cover. Poach for 6 minutes, or until the fish begins to flake. Carefully remove and set aside, discarding the milk.

2. In a large skillet over medium heat, cook the vegetable oil and onion for 8 to 10 minutes, or until soft and translucent. Add the garlic and cook 2 minutes. Add the curry powder, coriander (leaving a pinch for garnish), turmeric, cayenne, and rice, stirring to coat. Cook for 3 to 5 minutes. Remove from the heat and stir through the coriander and parsley. Season with salt and black pepper.

3. In a small bowl, combine the yoghurt with the lime juice and zest. Season well with salt and black pepper and set aside.

4. In a large frying pan over medium heat, add the olive oil and cook the eggs for 5 minutes, or until the whites have set and the yolks are warm.

5. To serve, divide the rice and fish among plates and top with a fried egg, a good dollop of yoghurt, and a sprinkling of fresh herbs.

TIP: *The rice mix and fish can both be made up to a day in advance and kept separately until ready to assemble.*

CHAPTER 2

soups

MUM'S CHICKEN SOUP

The smell of chicken soup on the stove makes me think of being wrapped up in a cozy blanket while home sick from school, watching afternoon TV. Though I was under the weather, these are nice memories because I felt coddled and cared for, and to this day chicken soup makes me feel nourished. Now, with a family of three children under the age of five, there is almost always someone with a sniffle, so I am perpetually making batches of Mum's Chicken Soup. **SERVES 10**

1 organic, free-range chicken (3–4 pounds)

1 onion, peeled and quartered

2 celery stalks, roughly chopped and divided

1 leek, thoroughly washed and roughly chopped

1 large carrot, peeled and roughly chopped, plus 2 carrots, peeled and diced

1 thumb-size piece of ginger, peeled and roughly chopped

1 bay leaf

2 sprigs thyme

1 small bunch parsley, stems and leaves chopped separately

2 teaspoons sea salt, plus more to taste

1 teaspoon black peppercorns

1 lemon, halved

1. In a large stockpot, combine the whole chicken, onion, half the celery, the leek, roughly chopped carrot, ginger, bay leaf, thyme, and parsley stems. Fill the pot with enough cold water to cover the chicken so it is submerged. Season with 2 teaspoons sea salt.

2. Bring the water to a boil over a high heat, then reduce to a simmer and cook the chicken for 2 hours, or until tender.

3. Strain the soup into a clean soup pot and discard the vegetables. Allow the chicken to cool slightly before picking apart the meat from the bones, both white and dark, and set aside.

4. Add the remaining celery and diced carrots to the fresh stock and return to the heat. Cook for 15 to 20 minutes, or until they are slightly tender, and then add the chicken. Season to taste with salt, peppercorns, fresh parsley leaves, and a good squeeze of lemon juice.

TIPS: *Make double the stock and store in the freezer to heat up later. (Use plastic or glass airtight containers, but leave room at the top as the soup will expand.)*

The key to good chicken soup is a good-quality chicken. Whenever possible, use an organic, free-range or corn-fed bird. I like to get mine from my butcher, Jago Butchers on Elystan Street in Chelsea.

MINESTRONE

This simple but satisfying soup is perfect for those damp winter days in London. Pureeing some of the soup gives it a thicker, more luxurious texture. It's a terrific vegetarian main with ample protein from the beans and greens. Feel free to replace the spinach with any other green you have in your fridge, such as kale, chard, or mustard leaves. **SERVES 6**

2 tablespoons olive oil

2 leeks, halved, washed, and finely sliced

1 onion, finely chopped

2 cloves garlic, minced

2 carrots, peeled and diced

2 sprigs thyme

½ bunch flat-leaf parsley, leaves and stalks separated and finely chopped

1 bay leaf

1 can (14 ounces) San Marzano tomatoes

4 cups Vegetable Stock (page 217)

Salt and ground black pepper, to taste

1 can (14 ounces) cannellini beans, rinsed and drained

1 bunch baby spinach leaves

Juice from half a lemon

1 cup grated Parmesan cheese, to serve

¼ cup basil leaves, to garnish

1. In a large stockpot over medium heat, cook the olive oil, leeks, and onion for 6 to 8 minutes, or until softened and translucent. Add the garlic and cook for 2 more minutes. Add the carrots, stirring, and cook for 5 minutes, or until they begin to soften.

2. Add the thyme, chopped parsley stalks, and bay leaf along with the tomatoes and vegetable stock. Season with salt and pepper. Bring to a boil, then reduce the heat and simmer for 25 minutes.

3. Add the beans and cook for another 10 minutes. Remove the thyme sprigs and bay leaf and carefully decant one-third of the soup into a large bowl or food processor. With either a hand blender or a food processor, blitz the soup until it's pureed. Pour the pureed soup back into the large pot with the remaining soup. Add the spinach and parsley leaves and cook for 5 minutes, or until wilted.

4. Right before serving, stir through the lemon juice. Divide into bowls and top with freshly grated Parmesan cheese, black pepper, and basil leaves.

TIP: *San Marzano tomatoes are my favourite to use in this soup, but any can of good-quality plum tomatoes will do just fine!*

GAZPACHO

This is a great soup for entertaining in the summertime, as it's quick to put together and best made ahead. The key to making a great gazpacho is super-fresh ingredients and good vinegar. My favourite is sherry vinegar from Spain, which has a particularly rich, full flavour, but an excellent substitute is apple cider vinegar. **SERVES 6**

½ **head garlic**

2 **red bell peppers, cut in half**

1 **cup plus 1 tablespoon olive oil, plus more for serving**

1 **onion, quartered**

Salt and ground black pepper, to taste

3 **cups roughly chopped ripe tomatoes**

1 **cucumber, peeled and chopped**

6 **tablespoons sherry vinegar**

2 **slices sourdough bread, torn**

Good squeeze of lemon juice

Large handful of basil leaves

Large handful of parsley leaves, plus extra to garnish

1. Preheat the oven to 400°F. Line a baking tray with parchment paper. Place the garlic and red peppers on the tray skin side up and drizzle with 1 tablespoon olive oil. Add the onion to the tray. Season with salt and pepper. Roast for 30 minutes, or until the peppers are softened and charred, the onion is soft, and you can squeeze the garlic from the skin.

2. Meanwhile, place the tomatoes, cucumber, vinegar, the remaining 1 cup olive oil, and the bread in a large bowl. Push the mixture down so the bread soaks up the vinegar and oil. Allow this to rest while the vegetables roast.

3. Once the vegetables have cooled down, place them in a food processor along with the bread-tomato mixture. Blitz until smooth, adding the lemon juice, basil, and parsley leaves. Season to taste.

4. Place the mixture in the refrigerator until chilled. Serve with a good drizzle of olive oil and parsley to garnish.

TIP: *You can sprinkle whatever you want on top of gazpacho—diced cucumbers, green peppers, red peppers, hard-boiled egg, and white onion are all delicious. I often dice up some toppings and put them on a side plate for my kids to add in what they want—they love to sprinkle their soup with their favourite additions.*

ROASTED BUTTERNUT SQUASH SOUP WITH CRISPY SAGE AND CASHEW CREAM

This is one of my favourite vegan suppers. It is so creamy and filling, my husband doesn't even complain that I'm starving him with healthy food. **SERVES 6**

1 butternut squash, peeled and cut into large chunks

1 sweet potato, peeled and cut into large chunks

4 tablespoons olive oil, divided

Salt and ground black pepper, to taste

2 leeks, washed thoroughly and thinly sliced

2 cloves garlic, minced

½ teaspoon chili flakes

1 apple, peeled and roughly chopped (I like to use Granny Smith)

4 cups Vegetable Stock (page 217)

8–10 sage leaves

Sea salt

Cashew Cream (page 212), to serve

TIP: *This soup is best made a day in advance to allow the flavours to intensify.*

1. Preheat the oven to 350°F. Line a large baking tray with parchment paper. Place the butternut squash and sweet potato on the tray and drizzle with 1 tablespoon of the olive oil. Season lightly with salt and black pepper. Roast for 35 to 45 minutes, or until tender and beginning to caramelize.

2. Meanwhile, in a large pot over medium heat, heat 1 tablespoon of the olive oil. Add the leeks and garlic and cook until softened, about 10 minutes. Add the chili flakes and apple, stirring to combine. Add the roasted squash and sweet potato along with the vegetable stock. Bring to a boil, then reduce to a simmer and cook for 25 minutes, or until the stock has reduced slightly.

3. With a hand blender or in a food processor, blitz the soup until smooth. Place back on a medium heat and cook for another 10 minutes until thickened, adding 1 to 2 cups of water if it's too thick. Season to taste with salt and black pepper.

4. In a small pan, heat the remaining 2 tablespoons olive oil. Carefully add the sage leaves and fry for 2 to 3 seconds on each side, or until they crisp up. Remove and drain on paper towels. Sprinkle with sea salt.

5. Divide the soup among 6 bowls. Top with the crispy sage leaves and dollops of Cashew Cream.

SPICY WHITE BEAN AND SQUASH SOUP WITH AVOCADO CREMA

Matt loves a spicy soup, and this one gets its kick from chipotle peppers. It's a batch soup that freezes well, which is great for tricky nights when I don't have time to cook but want something warm and full-flavoured. The avocado crema on top is laced with lime juice and adds a wonderful brightness to the dish. **SERVES 4**

1 tablespoon olive oil

1 red onion, chopped

2 cloves garlic, minced

4 sprigs coriander, leaves for garnish, stems left whole

1 teaspoon ground cumin

½ kabocha squash, peeled and roughly chopped (about 4 cups)

1 tablespoon chopped chipotle peppers

5 cups Vegetable Stock (page 217)

1 can (14 ounces) white beans, such as cannellini, rinsed and drained

Salt and ground black pepper, to taste

1 lime, to squeeze

Avocado Crema

2 ripe avocados, peeled and pitted

¼ cup lime juice

2 tablespoons coconut cream

¼ teaspoon salt

¼ cup toasted pumpkin seeds, for garnish

1. In a large pot over medium heat, heat the olive oil. Add the onion, garlic, coriander stems, and cumin and cook for 10 minutes, or until soft and fragrant. Add the squash and chipotle peppers and stir to combine. Add the stock, increase the heat, and simmer until the squash is soft, about 30 minutes. Add the beans and cook for another 5 minutes to heat through. Remove the coriander stems. Using a hand blender or a food processor, blend the soup until smooth. Season to taste with salt, black pepper, and lime juice.

2. *To make the crema:* Place the avocados, lime juice, coconut cream, and salt in a blender and process until thick, luscious, and smooth.

3. To serve, divide the soup among 4 bowls. Top with the Avocado Crema, coriander leaves, and pumpkin seeds.

TIP: *If you can't find kabocha squash, substitute butternut squash.*

PEA AND HAM HOCK SOUP

This is a classic British soup filled with hearty split peas and smoked ham. It takes a bit of time on the stove, but the depth of flavour in the end result is completely worth the hours of simmering. Reserve this recipe for a rainy Sunday when no one is too rushed and your family is home to enjoy the scent of the soup cooking in the kitchen.

SERVES 6 TO 8

Ham Hock Stock

1 smoked ham hock (ask your butcher for the pork knuckle), soaked overnight in cold water

1 onion, peeled and halved

2 cloves garlic

1 celery stalk, roughly chopped

1 bay leaf

1 small bunch parsley

2 sprigs thyme

Soup

2 cups green split peas, soaked in cold water

4 tablespoons butter

1 onion, finely chopped

2 cloves garlic, minced

10½ cups Ham Hock Stock

Salt and ground black pepper, to taste

1 lemon, juiced

Olive oil, for serving

Sourdough bread, for serving

1. *To make the stock:* Drain and rinse the ham hock. Place in a large pot with the halved onion, whole garlic cloves, celery, bay leaf, parsley, and thyme. Cover with cold water. Bring to a boil, then reduce to a simmer and cook, partially covered, for 2½ hours, or until the meat is tender and falling away from the bone.

2. Allow the hock to cool completely in the liquid before removing it and straining the stock through a fine-mesh sieve into a clean bowl. Shred the meat into bite-size pieces.

3. *To make the soup:* Rinse the soaked peas and drain them. In a large pot over medium heat, melt the butter, then add the chopped onion and minced garlic. Sauté for 10 minutes, or until softened and translucent. Add the drained peas along with the ham stock. Bring to a boil, then reduce to a simmer and cook for 30 to 45 minutes, or until the peas are very soft. Add more stock or water if needed.

4. Remove half of the soup and blitz in a food processor until smooth. Return to the pot of unblended soup along with the ham pieces. Season to taste with salt, black pepper, and lemon juice, and serve with a good lug of olive oil and crusty sourdough bread.

salads

ICEBERG WEDGE WITH A TWIST

This is a classic American recipe, but I prepare mine with a few modifications. I use a mix of yoghurt and buttermilk for a tangier dressing, and I incorporate a creamy Roquefort cheese for richness. Here in the UK we use what's called streaky bacon to garnish the salad, but you should feel free to substitute pancetta or regular bacon.

SERVES 8

½ cup plain yoghurt

½ cup buttermilk

Zest and juice from ½ lemon

1 tablespoon finely chopped chives

½ cup crumbled Roquefort cheese

Ground black pepper, to taste

1 tablespoon olive oil, divided

6 slices streaky bacon, cut into lardoons

1–2 slices good sourdough bread, torn into bite-size pieces

Salt, to taste

2 heads iceberg lettuce, cut into wedges

⅓ cup walnuts, toasted and roughly chopped

1. In a small bowl, whisk together the yoghurt, buttermilk, lemon zest, lemon juice, and chives. Gently stir through the Roquefort cheese and season with black pepper. Set aside.

2. In a small nonstick frying pan over medium heat, heat ½ tablespoon of the olive oil. Add the bacon and fry for 6 minutes, turning once, or until golden and crisp. Remove and set aside on paper towels to drain excess oil.

3. In the same pan, add the remaining ½ tablespoon olive oil along with the torn bread pieces. Cook for 6 to 8 minutes, stirring occasionally, or until golden brown and crispy. Season with salt.

4. To assemble the salad, drizzle the yoghurt dressing over the lettuce wedges. Sprinkle on the bacon and toasted walnuts and garnish with the croutons. Serve immediately.

KALE AND ROASTED CAULIFLOWER SALAD

My sister-in-law, Deb, is a vegetarian, so I always try to have something special for her because most of the time, the rest of us are eating a roast. This salad is very easy to make and absolutely delicious, and I often forgo my own carnivore meal and join my sister-in-law in this vegetarian delight. **SERVES 4**

1 small head cauliflower, leaves removed, cut into florets

2 tablespoons olive oil

1 tablespoon cumin seeds

Sea salt

Dressing

2 tablespoons tahini paste

2 tablespoons water

Zest and juice from 1 lemon

1 tablespoon honey

3 tablespoons olive oil

Salt and ground black pepper, to taste

1 large bunch kale, tough stalks removed, roughly chopped

¼ cup toasted pumpkin seeds

3 Medjool dates, pitted and roughly chopped

½ red onion, thinly sliced

1. Preheat the oven to 400°F. Line a rimmed baking tray with parchment paper. In a large bowl, toss together the cauliflower florets, olive oil, cumin seeds, and a good pinch of salt. Spread evenly onto the baking tray and roast for 20 to 25 minutes, or until golden and tender, turning halfway.

2. *To make the dressing:* In a small bowl, whisk together the tahini paste and water. Whisk in the lemon zest, lemon juice, honey, and olive oil. Season with salt and black pepper to taste.

3. Meanwhile, in a large bowl, combine the kale with a small pinch of salt and a few tablespoons of the dressing. Gently massage the leaves with your hands until they are glossy and tender, about 2 minutes. Place on the serving dish and sprinkle with the pumpkin seeds, dates, and red onion.

4. Add the roasted cauliflower to the kale. Dress the salad with the remaining tahini sauce and toss to coat.

FIG AND PECORINO SALAD

In late summer, I get that "back to school" feeling and look forward to returning to our daily routine and catching up with friends. We always end up hosting a few dinner parties in the autumn after being away from London during the summer vacation, and this salad anchors my menus. It is a simple, elegant starter and best made when figs are in season (late summer and early fall). **SERVES 6**

¼ cup pine nuts

3 cups wild arugula

2 cups mustard leaves

½ cup fresh basil

8–10 ripe black figs, halved or quartered

3½ ounces Pecorino cheese

Dressing

1 shallot, finely chopped

1 tablespoon balsamic vinegar

½ tablespoon Dijon mustard

1 teaspoon honey

¼ cup olive oil

Salt and ground black pepper, to taste

1. In a small frying pan over low heat, gently toast the pine nuts until golden brown. Allow to cool completely.

2. *Meanwhile, to make the dressing:* In a small bowl, whisk together the shallot, balsamic vinegar, Dijon, and honey. While whisking, gradually add the olive oil until thick and emulsified. Season with salt and black pepper to taste.

3. In a medium bowl, mix together the arugula, mustard leaves, and basil. Place on a serving platter and arrange the figs. With a speed peeler, shave the Pecorino cheese evenly over the salad. Sprinkle with the toasted pine nuts, drizzle the dressing over, and serve immediately.

HERBY COUSCOUS WITH SLOW-ROAST TOMATOES

My kids and my husband all love couscous, so this dish keeps everyone happy. It's a great salad to make even when tomatoes are not in their peak season, as the method of roasting them low and slow helps to release their natural sugars, making them deliciously sweet and enormously flavourful regardless of the quality of your produce. If you want a heartier meal, you can easily substitute a heavier grain, such as barley or farro, for the couscous. **SERVES 6**

1½ pounds cherry tomatoes, halved

2 red onions, peeled and cut into 8 wedges each

3 tablespoons olive oil

Salt and ground black pepper, to taste

3 cups Chicken Stock (page 215) or Vegetable Stock (page 217)

2½ cups pearl couscous (moghrabieh)

1 cup pitted, roughly chopped kalamata olives

2 cups finely chopped mixed herbs, such as basil, parsley, and mint

Juice of 1 lemon

¼ cup good-quality olive oil

Salt and ground black pepper, to taste

¾ cup feta cheese

1. Preheat the oven to 200°F. Line a baking tray with parchment paper. Place the cherry tomatoes, cut side up, on the baking tray along with the onion wedges. Drizzle with the olive oil and season with salt and pepper. Roast for 1 hour, or until caramelized, sticky, and sweet.

2. Meanwhile, bring the stock to a boil. Add the couscous and simmer for 6 minutes. Remove from the heat, cover, and allow to stand for 10 minutes to soak up all of the stock.

3. Spread the couscous on a large, clean baking tray to cool.

4. In a large bowl, combine the olives, chopped herbs, cooled couscous, onions, and cherry tomatoes. Add the lemon juice and olive oil, tossing to coat. Season with salt and pepper. Crumble over the feta cheese and serve.

TIP: *Couscous stores well, so double this recipe and make extra for lunches later in the week.*

WINTER GREENS SALAD

This is a beautifully subtle, nutritious salad that works terrifically as a side to just about anything. The best thing about winter greens such as radicchio is their bitterness and ability to cleanse the palate. You can substitute other greens if you prefer, but the idea is to keep it simple. **SERVES 6**

1 round radicchio, cored and thickly sliced

1 escarole, leaves loosely torn

10 Brussels sprouts, halved, then thinly sliced

1 cup baby arugula

½ cup Pecorino cheese, thinly shaved

½ cup walnuts, toasted and roughly chopped

Dressing

1 banana shallot, finely chopped

½ clove garlic, minced

1 teaspoon good-quality maple syrup

3 tablespoons apple cider vinegar

½ cup olive oil

Sea salt and ground black pepper, to taste

1. Combine the radicchio, escarole, Brussels sprouts, and arugula in a large serving bowl. Scatter the shaved pecorino and walnuts over the top.

2. *To make the dressing:* In a small bowl, whisk together the shallot, garlic, syrup, and vinegar. Gradually add the olive oil, whisking to emulsify. Season to taste with salt and black pepper.

3. Drizzle the dressing over the salad and serve immediately.

FRENCH BEAN AND SUGAR SNAP PEA NIÇOISE

This salad was inspired by a similar dish at a wonderful café in London called Ottolenghi, where Chef Yotam Ottolenghi creates beautiful, colourful salads with bold flavours. My twist is to make it more substantial, perfect for a complete lunch or a light dinner. In the UK, the name for a sugar snap pea is a *mange tout*—needless to say, when I first read a recipe that listed *mange tout,* I was completely thrown, thinking that it was a type of fish. Brits and Americans both speak English, but trust me when I say sometimes it feels like I'm hearing a completely foreign language!

SERVES 4 AS A MAIN DISH

8–10 small new potatoes

2 cups French beans

2 cups sugar snap peas

2 jars (3.95 ounces each) good-quality tuna packed in olive oil

⅓ cup blanched hazelnuts

Juice of 1 small orange

1 tablespoon lemon juice

1 clove garlic, minced

1 teaspoon honey

1 tablespoon hazelnut oil (optional)

3 tablespoons olive oil

Sea salt and ground black pepper, to taste

¼ cup finely chopped chives

2 tablespoons fresh tarragon leaves

1 cup cherry tomatoes, halved

1. Bring a large pot of salted water to a boil. Add the new potatoes and cook for about 15 minutes, or until fork-tender. Remove with a slotted spoon and allow to cool before slicing in half.

2. In the same pot of water, add the French beans and sugar snap peas and cook for 3 minutes. Drain and run under cold water until they have cooled. Pat dry.

3. While the beans are cooking, place the hazelnuts in a dry frying pan over medium heat. Toast them for 4 to 6 minutes, or until golden brown, then remove and roughly chop.

4. In a small bowl, whisk together the orange juice, lemon juice, garlic, honey, hazelnut oil (if using), and olive oil. Season the dressing with salt and pepper to taste.

5. To assemble the salad, mix the potatoes, beans, chives, tarragon, cherry tomatoes, and salad dressing, tossing to coat. Add the tuna in chunks, lightly toss together, and sprinkle with the hazelnuts. Serve with crusty bread.

NOTE: *This recipe makes about twice the amount of dressing needed, but I like to serve some on the side because some people like a bit more.*

PANZANELLA
(AKA JULIE'S BREAD SALAD)

My dear high school and college roommate, Julie Fenton, introduced me to this salad. We called it Bread Salad, and she would make it for Middlebury College tailgates (the bread would helpfully line our stomachs for the onslaught of Natty Light beer). Our love for Bread Salad even made its way onto her wedding menu, which made me one very happy bridesmaid. Years later, when Matt and I were traveling in Florence, I discovered that Julie's Bread Salad actually has a posh Italian cousin—panzanella!

SERVES 6

1 loaf day-old ciabatta or sourdough bread, cut into cubes

2 cloves garlic, minced

3 tablespoons olive oil

Salt and ground black pepper, to taste

1½ pounds mixed heirloom tomatoes, halved and quartered

1 cucumber, halved and sliced

1 red bell pepper, cored and thinly sliced

1 green bell pepper, cored and thinly sliced

1 large handful basil leaves

2 tablespoons capers, drained

2 anchovies, finely chopped

2 tablespoons red wine vinegar

5 tablespoons good-quality olive oil

½ cup almonds

1. Preheat the oven to 400°F. Line a baking tray with parchment paper. In a large bowl, toss together the bread cubes, garlic, and olive oil. Season with salt and black pepper. Spread onto the prepared baking tray and toast in the oven for 20 to 25 minutes, or until golden brown and crisp. Remove and allow to cool.

2. Place the almonds on the tray and roast for 10 minutes, or until fragrant. Cool then roughly chop.

3. In a large bowl, combine the tomatoes, cucumber, red and green pepper, and basil leaves.

4. In a small bowl, stir together the capers, anchovies, red wine vinegar, olive oil, and salt and pepper to taste. Add the almonds to the tomato mixture and pour the dressing over all, tossing to combine, then add the bread and mix thoroughly. Allow the salad to sit for at least half an hour before serving so the bread softens.

TIP: *I like to toast my bread even though it is day-old—it tends to hold better as the salad sits.*

CAULIFLOWER TABBOULEH WITH TOASTED NUT MIX

Cauliflower "rice" is a delicious vegan and grain-free substitute for wheat. London is blessed with an abundance of great Middle Eastern restaurants, and this is my version of one of the most common salads, tabbouleh. I like to add lots of nuts on top for texture and protein. **SERVES 6**

Toasted Nut Mix
1 teaspoon cumin seeds
1 teaspoon coriander seeds
¼ cup hazelnuts
¼ cup almonds
¼ cup cashews
2 teaspoons za'atar
Pinch of sea salt

Cauliflower Tabbouleh
1 head cauliflower, leaves removed, cut into florets

2–3 large tomatoes, deseeded and finely chopped
1 cucumber, deseeded and finely chopped
5–6 radishes, finely chopped
1 green bell pepper, finely chopped
4 green onions, thinly sliced on the bias
1 bunch mint leaves, shredded

1 bunch coriander leaves, finely chopped
1 bunch flat-leaf parsley, finely chopped
Zest and juice from 1 lemon
2 tablespoons good-quality olive oil
Sea salt and ground black pepper, to taste

1. *To make the nut mix:* Place the cumin and coriander seeds in a dry pan over medium heat. Roast for 2 to 3 minutes, or until fragrant, then pour into a mortar. Grind with a pestle until you have a powder. Add the hazelnuts, almonds, and cashews to the same pan and toast for 6 to 8 minutes, or until golden. Transfer to the mortar along with the za'atar and a pinch of sea salt. Using the pestle, roughly bash the nuts until they are chopped. Set aside to cool completely.

2. In batches, pulse the cauliflower florets in a food processor until a fine crumb has formed. Transfer to a steamer set over a pan of boiling water, cover, and steam for 2 to 3 minutes, until the cauliflower is cooked but still firm. Remove the steamer from the pan and leave to steam-dry and cool.

3. In a large bowl, combine the tomatoes, cucumber, radishes, green pepper, green onions, mint, coriander, and parsley with the cauliflower. Add the lemon zest, lemon juice, and olive oil. Season to taste with salt and pepper. Stir through the nut mix and serve.

TIP: *This stores well, so make a day in advance or double the recipe for leftovers later in the week.*

PORTOBELLO QUINOA CUPS

This is another Deb dish (my sister-in-law is a vegetarian), so when Deb comes over, she usually gets either the Kale and Roasted Cauliflower Salad (page 59) or this mushroom dish. And I often forgo the meaty dish to share this dish with her.

SERVES 3

1¾ cups water

1 cup quinoa

Salt

3 tablespoons balsamic vinegar

1 shallot, finely chopped

1 teaspoon honey

6 tablespoons olive oil

Ground black pepper, to taste

6 portobello mushrooms, cleaned

1 celery stalk, finely chopped

3 scallions, thinly sliced

1 cup wild arugula

1 pint cherry tomatoes, halved

3 tablespoons finely chopped fresh flat-leaf parsley plus additional for garnish

1 cup crumbled goat cheese, for garnish

1. In a medium saucepan over medium-high heat, combine the water, quinoa, and a pinch of salt. Bring to a boil, then reduce the heat, cover, and cook for 12 to 15 minutes, or until all of the water is absorbed and the quinoa has sprouted. Place a dry paper towel between the pan and the lid and set aside for at least 5 minutes before fluffing with a fork.

2. Preheat a grill pan or your grill. In a small bowl, whisk together the balsamic vinegar, shallot, honey, olive oil, and salt and pepper to taste. Lay the mushrooms on a rimmed baking tray and spoon half of the marinade onto them, allowing them to sit while the grill preheats. Grill the mushrooms for 8 to 10 minutes, basting with the marinade and turning halfway through, or until soft and charred.

3. In a large bowl, mix together the reserved quinoa, celery, scallions, arugula, cherry tomatoes, and parsley. Add the remainder of the mushroom marinade, tossing to coat. Season with salt and pepper to taste.

4. To serve, top the mushrooms with the quinoa salad and garnish with goat cheese and additional parsley.

speedy sides

CUCUMBER SALAD

This is a light, refreshing salad to serve alongside roasts or even as a starter. I like to use small cucumbers, sometimes called Persian cucumbers, rather than the standard English ones. Try them if you can find them in your local shop, as they have fewer seeds and are crisper and sweeter. **SERVES 6**

8–10 small cucumbers, each about 4 to 5 inches in length

2 tablespoons extra virgin olive oil

Zest and juice from 1 lemon

1 tablespoon nigella seeds, plus extra to serve

½ cup plain Greek yoghurt

Salt and ground black pepper, to taste

2 tablespoons tahini paste

2 teaspoons water

1 clove garlic, grated

Salt and ground black pepper, to taste

1 tablespoon fresh dill leaves

1 cup mâche or pea shoots

1. Using a speed peeler, peel the cucumbers into long strips.

2. In a large bowl, toss the cucumber strips with the olive oil, lemon zest and juice, nigella seeds, and 1 tablespoon of the yoghurt. Season well with salt and pepper.

3. In a small bowl, whisk together the tahini paste with the water. Add the remaining yoghurt and grated garlic and season with salt and pepper.

4. To serve, spread the yoghurt mixture on a plate, combine the cucumber with the dill and mâche, and pile it on top. Sprinkle with the remaining nigella seeds and serve.

ROASTED BEETROOTS

I'll never forget the first time I was cooking in London and the recipe I was using called for "beetroot." I was at the supermarket looking all over for whatever this beetroot might be. After finally resorting to Google, I discovered this word was simply the UK translation of my favourite "beet."

Beets, plain and simple. They are roasted here with a zingy marinade and make the perfect colourful side for any roast. **SERVES 4 TO 6**

1 bunch mixed-colour
  beetroots with
  leaves
3 tablespoons olive oil,
  divided
Salt and ground black
  pepper, to taste
1 orange, segmented
  and juice reserved
1 tablespoon apple
  cider vinegar
1 teaspoon honey
2 tablespoons fresh
  mint leaves, thinly
  shredded
¼ cup hazelnuts,
  toasted and
  roughly chopped
½ cup soft goat cheese

1. Preheat the oven to 400°F. Line a baking tray with parchment paper.

2. Peel the beetroots and cut into small wedges. Place in a large bowl along with 1 tablespoon of the olive oil, salt, and pepper. Toss to combine, then tip onto the baking tray. Roast in the oven for 30 to 35 minutes, or until tender.

3. Meanwhile, in a separate bowl, whisk together the remaining 2 tablespoons olive oil, the orange juice, vinegar, and honey. Add the roasted, warm beetroots, toss them in the dressing, and allow them to sit until they have come to room temperature.

4. To finish, season with additional salt and pepper, toss with the mint, and then tip onto a platter and serve with a sprinkling of hazelnuts, orange pieces, and goat cheese.

COLESLAW

My husband loves coleslaw and would eat it every day. To defend his waistline, I like to swap out the traditional mayonnaise in the dressing for a mix of yoghurt and crème fraîche. It's lighter, tangier, and healthier. This is a great salad to prepare ahead of time for a crowd and toss before serving. I like the vegetables to stay nice and crunchy, and the addition of fresh herbs and toasted nuts gives it that extra oomph. **SERVES 6**

¼ cup sour cream or crème fraîche

¼ cup plain yoghurt

Zest and juice from 1 lime

1 teaspoon honey

Salt and ground black pepper, to taste

¼ red cabbage, thinly shredded

¼ white cabbage, thinly shredded

2 large carrots, peeled and thinly julienned

¼ red onion, thinly sliced

2 spring onions, thinly sliced on the bias

½ cup finely chopped chives

½ cup finely chopped flat-leaf parsley

½ cup walnut pieces, lightly toasted

1. In a small bowl, whisk together the sour cream or crème fraîche, yoghurt, lime zest, lime juice, and honey. Season with salt and pepper and set aside.

2. In a large bowl, combine the cabbages, carrots, red onion, and spring onions. Add the dressing and toss to combine. Tip onto a platter and sprinkle with the chives, parsley, and walnuts. Serve immediately.

ROAST SWEET POTATO AND FETA SALAD

I often make my kids sweet potato fries, and this dish came about when I roasted too many. (Actually, we can never have too many sweet potato fries!) I add a bit of saltiness with the cheese and freshness with the citrus and herbs, and presto!—a side for Mummy and Daddy's supper.

This salad is great when you have extra veggies kicking around and need something simple yet satisfying. **SERVES 4–6**

4 small sweet potatoes

1 tablespoon tomato paste

1 tablespoon brown sugar

2 teaspoons paprika

1 clove garlic, grated

4 tablespoons olive oil, divided

Salt and ground black pepper, to taste

1 tablespoon lime juice

1 tablespoon fresh marjoram leaves, roughly chopped

½ cup pistachios, roughly chopped

1 celery stalk, thinly sliced

½ cup cubed feta cheese

1. Preheat the oven to 400°F. Line a baking tray with parchment paper.

2. Scrub the potatoes well, then halve them lengthwise and cut each similarly into 5 long wedges.

3. In a large bowl, combine the tomato paste, brown sugar, paprika, garlic, and 2 tablespoons of olive oil, mixing well. Add the sweet potatoes, tossing to coat. Place on the baking tray and toss with 1 teaspoon of the olive oil. Season with salt and pepper, and roast for 30 to 35 minutes, or until caramelized and tender. Remove and allow to cool.

4. In a small bowl, whisk the remaining olive oil with the lime juice and season with salt and pepper.

5. Place the potato pieces on a platter. Scatter the marjoram, pistachios, celery, and cheese over the potatoes. Drizzle with the dressing and serve.

TIP: *For an extra kick, slice 1 jalapeño into thin rounds and scatter on top.*

NEW POTATO SALAD

Matt is happiest if he has potatoes at every meal—a true Brit! So I'm always making this salad. The trick to taking this dish over-the-top is to dress the potatoes with the vinaigrette while they are still warm. That way, they soak up all the lovely bits of dressing and become infused with flavour. Leave them to cool to room temperature and then dig in. **SERVES 8**

1 tablespoon grainy mustard

2 anchovies, finely chopped

1 tablespoon champagne vinegar

1 teaspoon lemon zest plus 1 tablespoon lemon juice

1 teaspoon honey

¼ cup olive oil

Salt and ground black pepper, to taste

1 pound new potatoes

2 tablespoons finely chopped chives

1 tablespoon finely chopped dill

1. In a bowl, whisk together the mustard, anchovies, vinegar, lemon zest, lemon juice, honey, and olive oil. Season with salt and pepper to taste.

2. Bring a large pot of salted water to a boil over medium-high heat. Add the potatoes and cook for 10 to 12 minutes, or until fork-tender. Drain and carefully, while hot, slice in half. Place in a large bowl and toss with the dressing. Leave to cool to room temperature before sprinkling with the fresh chives and dill.

RADISH AND BROAD BEAN SALAD

Clean and refreshing, this salad is the perfect companion to a heavy dish. I like to use frozen broad beans because they are available year-round, but if you can get your hands on the fresh ones, then by all means use them. To save time (and patience), I remove the thin outer skins from only half of the broad beans. The leftover beans lend a nice texture and colour variation to the salad in any case. Kefir is a gut-healthy addition to the dressing that is creamy but light. **SERVES 4**

2 cups frozen broad beans

4 tablespoons kefir (or substitute 3 tablespoons natural plain yoghurt and 1 tablespoon buttermilk)

1 teaspoon blossom honey

1 tablespoon lemon juice

1 tablespoon olive oil

Salt and ground black pepper, to taste

1 cup thinly sliced French radishes

1. Bring a large pot of water to a boil. Add the frozen beans and cook for 1 to 2 minutes, or until they begin to soften. Drain and immediately place in an ice bath or run under cold water. Lay onto paper towels to drain completely. Remove the skins from half of the beans to reveal the gorgeous green beans.

2. In a small bowl, whisk together the kefir (or yoghurt and buttermilk substitute), honey, lemon juice, olive oil, salt, and pepper.

3. In a medium bowl, combine the radishes with the beans, adding half the dressing to coat.

4. Tip onto a small platter and serve the remaining dressing on the side.

classic comforts

TOAD IN THE HOLE

Traditionally made with whatever leftover meat was on hand, Toad in the Hole has evolved into a stick-to-your-ribs dish of sausages encased in fluffy batter. I like to brown the sausages before folding them into the batter, which makes for a slightly more labour-intensive meal—but it looks even more irresistible. My family requests this on Sunday evenings; it's a very cozy, comforting supper. **SERVES 4**

3 tablespoons lard, divided

8 mild-flavoured sausages

4 large eggs

1 cup flour, sifted

1⅓ cups whole milk

1 tablespoon grainy mustard

1 teaspoon salt

Leaves from 2 sprigs rosemary

Freshly ground black pepper, to taste

1. Preheat the oven to 450°F. In a large frying pan over medium heat, melt 1 tablespoon of the lard. Fry the sausages until browned on all sides. Set the pan aside.

2. In a large bowl, whisk the eggs until light and fluffy, about 4 minutes. Add the flour and gradually pour in the milk, whisking to combine until smooth. Stir through the mustard and salt, then allow the mixture to sit for 10 minutes. Let the batter rest for at least 30 minutes.

3. In a rectangular ovenproof 10-inch x 8-inch roasting pan, add the remaining 2 tablespoons lard and place in the oven for 10 minutes to heat up. Carefully remove and quickly place over a medium heat. Add the fat from the sausage pan along with the batter. Arrange the sausages on top and sprinkle with rosemary leaves and pepper. Place in the oven and bake for 25 to 35 minutes, or until golden brown and puffed. Serve immediately with Chili Minted Peas (page 129).

CHILI CON CARNE

Chili is one of the most popular comfort foods in my household. It's a gift to busy home cooks: a great batch recipe that can easily be made ahead and frozen for a later date. I love the smokiness from the chipotle chili and warming heat from the spices. You can replace the beef with ground chicken or turkey to lighten things up if you wish. Apparently, it is a British tradition (or one that my husband grew up with) to pour chili over pasta—but I've suggested my favourite accompaniment, brown rice.

SERVES 6 TO 8

2 tablespoons olive oil

2 red onions, thinly sliced

2 medium carrots, peeled and diced

2 celery stalks, diced

2 cloves garlic, minced

1 red bell pepper, diced

1 teaspoon ground cumin

1 teaspoon paprika

1 tablespoon finely chopped chipotle chili

1 jalapeño chili, deseeded and finely chopped

1 pound lean ground beef

2 cans (14 ounces each) crushed tomatoes

1¼ cups Chicken Stock (page 215) or beef stock

Salt and ground black pepper, to taste

3 cups brown basmati rice, rinsed

1 lime, zest peeled with speed peeler and cut into wedges

1. In a large casserole pan over medium heat, heat the olive oil. Add the onions and cook for 10 minutes, or until softened, translucent, and slightly golden. Add the carrots, celery, garlic, and red pepper, cooking for another 5 minutes. Add the cumin, paprika, chipotle, and jalapeño, stirring to combine.

2. Add the beef, breaking it up with a spoon. Cook for 5 minutes, or until it begins to brown, then add the crushed tomatoes and stock. Season with salt and pepper, bring to a boil, and then reduce to a simmer. Partially cover with a lid and cook gently for an hour, stirring every so often.

3. Meanwhile, in a medium saucepan, combine the rice with 6 cups water. Add a pinch of salt and a strip of lime zest. Bring to a boil, then cover and reduce to a simmer. Cook for 25 to 30 minutes, or until the water is fully absorbed and the rice is tender. Remove from the heat and set aside until ready to serve.

4. When the chili is almost done, add the beans and heat through.

1 can (15½ ounces)
   white cannellini
   beans (for colour),
   rinsed and drained
1 diced avocado,
   to serve
½ cup sour cream,
   to serve
½ cup fresh coriander
   leaves, to serve

5. Divide the rice among bowls and top with the chili. Garnish with avocado, dollops of sour cream, fresh coriander, and lime wedges.

TIP: *To make a kiddie version, I just leave out the chili spices. My husband will always add some spice or chopped jalapeños to his dish, but for a more family-friendly version, I leave the spices out.*

MUSHROOM AND TARRAGON PIE

Handmade savoury pies are a long-standing tradition in the UK, and you can find them at just about any pub. The flaky, buttery pastry filled with rich stew makes for the perfect supper when served with a green salad. The best part about homemade pie (or mostly homemade—I use store-bought pastry in this recipe, which is sometimes the best option for a busy mom) is that it can be made ahead and frozen, so the only thing left to do is to pop it into the oven to bake. This vegetarian pie is a firm favourite in my household. The béchamel may seem very thick, but it's necessary—the addition of mushrooms and leeks makes the filling quite liquid, so you need the base to be thick! **SERVES 8**

½ cup unsalted butter, divided

¼ cup all-purpose flour, plus more to dust

2 cups whole milk, at room temperature

Salt and ground black pepper, to taste

1 tablespoon Dijon mustard

Juice from half a lemon

2 tablespoons tarragon, leaves picked and roughly chopped

3 tablespoons crème fraîche (or substitute sour cream)

1 leek, cleaned thoroughly, halved, and thinly sliced

1 clove garlic, minced

5 cups mixed mushrooms, cleaned and roughly chopped (I like to use white, brown, and chestnut)

1. In a medium saucepan over low heat, melt ¼ cup of butter, then add the flour. Stir for a couple minutes, then remove from the heat and gradually whisk in the milk until smooth. Do this carefully. It may start to form clumps, but just keep whisking! Season with salt and pepper.

2. Increase the heat to medium, continually whisking, allowing the mixture to come to a boil. Reduce the heat to a simmer and whisk vigorously as the mixtures thickens to "cook" the flour. Stir through the mustard, lemon juice, tarragon leaves, and crème fraîche (or sour cream). Taste for seasoning and set aside.

3. Melt the remaining butter in a frying pan over medium heat. Add the leek and sauté for 5 minutes, or until it begins to turn translucent. Add the garlic and continue cooking until fragrant. Increase the heat and add the mushrooms, cooking for 10 to 12 minutes, until all of the water they released has evaporated. Once the mushrooms have finished, add the kale and cook for 2 minutes until just wilted. You can add a dash of water at this point if needed. Remove from the heat and allow the mixture to cool slightly before stirring into the white sauce.

recipe continues

4 cups shredded kale

½ pound store-bought puff pastry

1 egg yolk, beaten with 2 teaspoons milk

4. Place the filling in a 10-inch x 8-inch pie dish and allow to cool completely.

5. Preheat the oven to 400°F. On a lightly floured surface, roll out your pastry to ¼-inch thickness. Brush the lip of the pie dish with the beaten egg yolk, then place the pastry on top, pressing firmly. Crimp the edges with your fingers or a fork.

6. Make 3 slits in the pastry to allow steam to escape. Brush the top with the remaining egg wash. Bake for 30 to 35 minutes, or until the pastry is golden brown. Allow to cool for 10 minutes before serving.

TIP: *For the carnivores in your household, you can add 1 pound of cooked, shredded chicken to the filling.*

FISH PIE

Fish Pie is one of the most-loved dishes at Bumpkin, our restaurant, and also one of my favourite meals. A traditional British recipe, this is a supper to keep in your back pocket for a dreary November evening. You can use any kind of fish or seafood, but I love the combination of smoked flaky white fish, salmon, and prawns. Always use more fish than seafood. **SERVES 6**

Potato Mash
2 pounds floury potatoes, peeled and cut into large chunks
2 tablespoons butter
Salt and ground black pepper, to taste

Sauce
3 tablespoons butter
1 shallot, finely chopped
3 tablespoons flour
¾ cup plus 1 tablespoon whole milk
1¼ cups Fish Stock (page 218)
1 clove garlic
1 bay leaf
1 anchovy, finely chopped
½ cup crème fraîche or sour cream

1. Preheat the oven to 350°F.

2. *To make the potato mash:* Place the potatoes in a large pot and cover with water. Bring to a boil, then simmer for 20 minutes, or until tender. Drain and place back into the pan with the butter. Mash until smooth, season with salt and pepper, and set aside.

3. *To make the sauce:* In a saucepan over medium heat, melt the butter and add the shallot, cooking for 5 minutes, or until softened. Add the flour and stir to combine. Cook for 2 to 3 minutes before gradually adding the milk and fish stock, whisking until smooth. Add the whole garlic clove, bay leaf, and anchovy. Reduce to a simmer and cook for 15 minutes, or until thickened. Season with salt and pepper and remove from the heat. Stir through the crème fraîche. Remove and discard the bay leaf and garlic clove.

4. *To make the pie:* In a large frying pan over medium heat, add the butter and onion. Cook for 15 minutes, or until softened and translucent. Add the haddock and salmon and fry for 2 to 3 minutes. This helps to remove some of the moisture so the sauce doesn't get too thin when cooking.

recipe continues

Pie

3 tablespoons butter

1 onion, finely chopped

1 pound smoked haddock, cut into chunks (you may need to preorder from your fishmonger as it isn't always readily available)

½ pound salmon, cut into chunks

½ pound large prawns, deveined and shells removed

¼ cup flat-leaf parsley leaves, finely chopped

½ cup grated Parmesan cheese

5. Transfer the fish to a large bowl. Pour over the sauce and add the prawns, onions, and parsley, stirring to combine. Tip into an 8½-inch x 7½-inch x 3-inch baking dish. Evenly top with the mash and sprinkle with the Parmesan. Bake for 30 minutes, or until golden and bubbling. Serve with Chili Minted Peas (page 129).

SWEET POTATO SHEPHERD'S PIE

This is my tried-and-true version of the classic family recipe. Though traditionally made with lamb mince, you can substitute beef if you prefer (this is called Cottage Pie). Sweet potato adds a nice vibrant colour and is packed full of natural sweetness and nutrients, perfect for the munchkins. **SERVES 8**

2 pounds large sweet potatoes, peeled and cut into large chunks

3 tablespoons butter, divided

Salt and ground black pepper, to taste

1 tablespoon olive oil

1 large Vidalia or other sweet onion, chopped

1 clove garlic, minced

2 carrots, peeled and chopped

1 celery stalk, chopped

1 tablespoon tomato paste

1½ pounds lean lamb mince

1 teaspoon ground cinnamon

Leaves from 3 sprigs fresh thyme, finely chopped

Leaves from 1 sprig fresh rosemary, finely chopped

1 tablespoon flour

1¼ cups Chicken Stock (page 215)

1. Place the potatoes in a large saucepan. Cover with cold water and a pinch of salt. Bring to a boil over medium heat, and cook until tender, about 20 minutes. Drain and place back into the pan with 2 tablespoons of the butter. Using an electric whisk, blend the potato and butter until smooth and season well with salt and pepper.

2. Preheat the oven to 350°F. In a large sauté pan over medium heat, add the remaining butter and the oil along with the onion. Cook for 15 minutes, or until softened and browned. Add the garlic, carrots, and celery, cooking for 6 to 8 minutes, or until softened. Stir through the tomato paste and cook for 1 minute, then remove from the pan and set aside.

3. Increase the heat and add the lamb mince, breaking it up with a wooden spoon, until browned, 5 to 6 minutes. Add the vegetables back to the pan along with the cinnamon, thyme, and rosemary. Stir to combine, then add the flour and cook for 1 minute. Add the stock and bring to a boil. Reduce the heat and simmer for 20 minutes, or until thickened. Check for seasoning.

4. Transfer the mixture to a 10-inch x 7-inch baking dish. Top evenly with the sweet potato mash and bake for 30 minutes, or until the filling is hot and bubbling and the sweet potato is beginning to darken where it peaks. Serve with Winter Greens Salad (page 64).

TIP: *This can be made ahead, frozen, and defrosted overnight in the fridge before it's baked in the oven.*

VEGETARIAN CURRY

There is nothing more warming than a curry. Matt always wants one when he comes home from a shoot, and I love a veggie curry if we are staying in on a Friday night. Just add a box set and a comfy couch and colour me happy! With this recipe, just toss in whatever you have in your veggie drawer in the fridge. Mine always takes on a different shape depending on what I want to use up. **SERVES 4**

1 medium eggplant, cut into 12 wedges

1 teaspoon sea salt

1 teaspoon cumin seeds

2 teaspoon coriander seeds

1 teaspoon ground turmeric

1 tablespoon fresh ginger, peeled and minced

2 cloves garlic, peeled and minced

2 tablespoons coconut oil

Salt and ground black pepper, to taste

1 onion, finely chopped

1 small tomato, roughly chopped

¼ cup coriander leaves, stalks finely chopped and leaves reserved

½ to 1 green chili, deseeded and finely chopped

2 teaspoons tamarind paste

1 tablespoon light brown sugar

1 can coconut milk

1 cup water

½ small head of cauliflower, cut into florets

1 cup broccolini, trimmed and cut into about 1-inch pieces

1 cup green beans, sliced on the bias

1 lime, cut in wedges to serve

Quinoa
2 cups quinoa

3 cups water

Pinch of salt

Cucumber Pickle
2 small cucumbers, sliced into thin rounds

1 tablespoon mirin

1. Place the eggplant in a medium bowl and sprinkle the salt over top. Allow to sit for 30 minutes, then lightly rinse and dry well.

2. In a small pan over medium heat, toast the cumin and coriander seeds for 2 minutes until fragrant. Transfer to a mortar and pestle and crush until ground. Stir through the turmeric, ginger, garlic, and a pinch of salt.

3. In a large pan over medium heat, cook 1 tablespoon of coconut oil and the onion for 4 to 6 minutes, or until soft and beginning to golden. Stir through the salt and pepper and cook for 1 minute. Add the eggplant, tomatoes, and remaining 1 tablespoon of oil and sauté for 2 to 3 minutes per side. Add the coriander stalks, chili, tamarind paste, and sugar. Add the coconut milk and water. Bring to a boil over medium heat, then reduce the heat and simmer for 15 minutes until the mixture begins to thicken and the eggplant is softening.

4. In a medium saucepan over medium heat, add the quinoa, water, and salt. Bring to a boil, then lower the heat to a simmer. Cover and cook for about 15 minutes, until all of the liquid is absorbed. Turn off the heat, place a dry paper towel between the pot and its lid, and let the quinoa sit for at least 3 minutes.

5. *Meanwhile, to make the cucumber pickle:* Place the sliced cucumber and mirin in a small bowl, tossing to coat. Set aside.

6. Once the eggplant has softened, add the cauliflower and broccolini to the curry. Cover and cook for 5 minutes until they begin to soften, add the green beans, and cook another 3 minutes. Remove from the heat, sprinkle with coriander leaves, and check seasoning.

7. Serve the curry on cooked quinoa with the pickled cucumber and lime wedges.

STEAMED MEDITERRANEAN FISH PARCELS

Not all comfort foods need to be rich and indulgent—sometimes comfort can mean simple, fresh, familiar flavours. These easy fish parcels are great for a quick supper and are even elegant enough for entertaining. **SERVES 4**

2 tablespoons olive oil

1 clove garlic, sliced

16 cherry tomatoes, halved

8 kalamata olives, pitted and roughly chopped

1 tablespoon capers

Sea salt and ground black pepper, to taste

4 fillets (6 ounces each) sea bass (or another flaky white fish)

1 small lemon, thinly sliced

4 tablespoons white wine

1 small bunch basil, leaves torn

1. Preheat the oven to 400°F. Cut 4 large squares of parchment paper.

2. In a skillet over medium heat, add 1 tablespoon oil. Add the garlic, cherry tomatoes, olives, and capers. Sauté for 3 minutes, or until the ingredients begin to soften. Season with salt and pepper and set aside.

3. Place a fish fillet in the centre of each piece of parchment. Arrange a lemon slice on top of each fillet and evenly divide the tomatoes, olives, and capers among the fish parcels. Sprinkle with a pinch of sea salt and pepper. Drizzle with 1 teaspoon olive oil and 1 tablespoon white wine.

4. Wrap each parcel by folding the sides together and creating a tent, ensuring there are no gaps as you fold the paper together.

5. Place the parcels on a baking sheet and bake for 8 to 10 minutes, or until the fish flakes easily and the flesh is opaque. Sprinkle the opened parcels with basil leaves, and serve immediately with Roasted Winter Vegetables (page 135).

STEAK AND ALE PIE

Though I'm a California girl at heart, I occasionally find myself yearning for London's weather to turn colder so we can cozy around the table with a warming Steak and Ale Pie. It is no wonder that it is a quintessentially British meal. I give the dish a lot of credit for keeping Brits from moving abroad!

This recipe requires a bit more effort because of the homemade pastry, but the end result is worthwhile, and it is a great activity to do with your kids on the weekend. The pastry can be made up to 2 days in advance. Allow it to soften slightly before rolling it out.

If you want to skip the pastry, you can serve the filling as a hearty stew. **MAKES 6 INDIVIDUAL PIES, SERVES 6**

Pastry

4½ cups all-purpose flour, sifted

½ cup cold butter, cut into cubes

½ cup cold lard, cut into cubes

¾ cup plus 1 tablespoon cold water

Filling

2 tablespoons butter

3 tablespoons olive oil

2½ pounds braising meat such as skirt steak, cut into ¾-inch pieces

1 large onion, chopped

2 large carrots, peeled and chopped

1 tablespoon tomato paste

1 teaspoon sugar

¼ cup flour

2½ cups sliced chestnut or brown mushrooms

1. *To make the pastry:* Place the flour in a large bowl. Add the butter and lard, and using your fingers, rub them into the flour until it resembles bread crumbs. Add the cold water, bringing together the mixture with your hands. Tip onto a clean surface and knead three times before wrapping in cling film and refrigerating for at least 30 minutes.

2. Preheat the oven to 275°F.

3. *To make the filling:* In a large, heavy-bottomed casserole pot, melt 1 tablespoon of the butter with 1 tablespoon of oil and add half of the braising meat, cooking for 2 to 3 minutes per side, or until golden brown. Remove and set aside. Repeat to cook the remaining beef. Add the onion and carrots to the pot with the remaining tablespoon of oil and cook, stirring, for 15 minutes, or until softened. Add the tomato paste, sugar, and flour, stirring for 2 to 3 minutes. Add the beef and any juices back to the pan along with the mushrooms. Deglaze with the ale and add the beef stock. Tie the thyme, bay leaf, and parsley together with some kitchen twine and place in the pot. Season with salt and pepper. Bake in the oven, covered, for 2 hours, or until the beef is tender. Allow to cool completely.

recipe continues

**1¼ cups ale (I prefer a
  sweeter ale, which
  gives better flavour
  to the gravy, so try
  Fuller's Golden
  Pride)**

**2 cups plus
  1½ tablespoons
  beef stock**

2–3 sprigs thyme

1 bay leaf

2 parsley stalks

**Salt and ground black
  pepper, to taste**

**1 egg yolk, beaten with
  1 tablespoon water**

4. When you're ready to bake the pies, heat the oven to 400°F. Grease six 1-cup ovenproof pie dishes. With a slotted spoon, divide the beef mixture among the pie dishes. You want it to come quite high, just above the edge. Discard the herbs. Add a little bit more of the beef gravy to the dish if need be, but do not fill up the entire way, as it will become soggy.

5. Divide the dough into 6 equal pieces. Roll out each piece on a lightly floured surface until it is large enough to cover the pastry dish and about ⅙-inch thick. Brush the edge of the pastry in the dish with egg wash, then carefully lift the pastry lid on top. Gently press around the edges and trim the extra pastry with a small knife. Using your thumb and index finger, gently crimp the edge of the pie all the way around. Brush with the egg wash and make 4 small slits in the centre of the pie to allow steam to escape.

6. Bake for 35 to 40 minutes, or until golden and crisp. Allow to rest for 10 minutes before serving with the remaining gravy.

TURKEY MEATBALLS AND SPAGHETTI

I first started making these for my eldest son when he was just old enough for adult food, so they have special significance in our kitchen. Ground turkey is a leaner option than beef, which is useful for me as I often end up eating dinner with the children and then another meal with my husband later in the evening. Skip the spaghetti for an easy, finger-food picnic supper. **SERVES 6 TO 8**

1 tablespoon olive oil, plus extra for greasing and drizzling

1 red onion, thinly sliced

1 clove garlic, minced

1 teaspoon chili flakes

6 ounces pancetta, diced

2 pounds ground turkey

6 oil-packed sun-dried tomatoes, finely chopped

½ cup flat-leaf parsley, finely chopped, plus extra to serve

½ cup finely chopped basil leaves

1½ cups bread crumbs

2 eggs, lightly beaten

1 cup grated Pecorino cheese, plus extra to serve

Salt and ground black pepper, to taste

Classic Tomato Sauce (page 214)

1 pound spaghetti

1. Preheat the oven to 350°F, and grease two nonstick baking sheets with a little oil.

2. Place a large sauté pan over medium heat and add the olive oil and onion. Cook for 10 minutes, or until beginning to caramelize. Add the garlic and chili flakes, cooking for a minute or so until fragrant. Tip into a small bowl and set aside to cool.

3. In the same pan, add the pancetta and cook for 6 to 8 minutes, or until golden. Transfer to another bowl and set aside to cool.

4. In a large bowl, combine the cooled onion mixture, cooled pancetta, ground turkey, sun-dried tomatoes, parsley, basil, bread crumbs, eggs, and Pecorino. Using your hands, mix everything together until well combined. Season with salt and pepper.

5. Using slightly wet hands, take golf ball–size portions of the mix and roll into balls. Place about 1 inch apart on the baking trays. Drizzle a little olive oil over the balls.

6. Bake for 20 to 25 minutes, or until golden brown, switching the trays when halfway through so they brown evenly. Meanwhile, pour the tomato sauce into a large pot and warm over low heat. Transfer the meatballs to the pot.

recipe continues

7. Bring a large pot of salted water to a boil. Add the pasta and cook according to package instructions. Drain well.

8. Divide the pasta into portions and top with the turkey meatballs and Classic Tomato Sauce (page 214). Garnish with Pecorino cheese and parsley.

TIP: *The meatballs can be made ahead of time, frozen for up to 1 month, and defrosted overnight in the fridge before baking. Gluten-free? Swap out the bread crumbs for ground almonds as a gluten-free binder.*

MAC AND CHEESE

Mac and cheese was one of my favourite childhood treats—but it has grown up with me, and the version below is for the adults. A mix of four rich and gooey cheeses with a touch of truffle oil transforms this otherwise simple pasta bake into a luxurious dinner-party standby. I serve this to our friends often, and it is a *major* crowd pleaser.

SERVES 6

1 pound macaroni

4 tablespoons butter, divided, plus extra for greasing

½ cup panko bread crumbs

1 tablespoon fresh thyme leaves, finely chopped

¼ cup grated Parmesan cheese

1 shallot, finely chopped

3 tablespoons flour

4 cups whole milk

Pinch of ground nutmeg

2 teaspoons Dijon mustard

4 ounces white Cheddar cheese, grated

4 ounces Fontina cheese, grated

3 ounces Gruyère cheese, grated

½–1 teaspoon truffle oil

Salt and ground black pepper, to taste

1. Preheat the oven to 375°F.

2. In a large saucepan of boiling salted water, cook the pasta until al dente. Drain well.

3. Meanwhile, melt 2 tablespoons of the butter in a large frying pan over medium heat. Add the panko bread crumbs and toast until golden brown. Remove from the heat and stir through the thyme and Parmesan cheese. Set aside.

4. In a large saucepan over medium heat, melt the remaining 2 tablespoons butter and add the shallot, cooking for 5 minutes, or until soft. Add the flour, stirring until well combined. Cook out the flour for 2 minutes before gradually whisking in the milk. Over low heat, whisk until thickened, then remove and season with nutmeg. Stir through the mustard and cheeses, whisking well to combine. Add the macaroni and fold through the truffle oil.

5. Butter an 8½-inch x 7½-inch x 3-inch baking dish and tip in the macaroni mixture. Sprinkle over the panko crumb mixture and bake for 25 to 30 minutes, or until golden and bubbling.

MAC AND CHEESE FOR KIDS

Macaroni and cheese is a great opportunity for getting some greens into your kids' meals. I like to cook broccoli or any other greens I have on hand, give them a whiz in the food processor, and then mix them into the white sauce. Not only do kids love the colour (green pasta!), but it's an easy, nutritious addition.

½ pound macaroni

1 head broccoli, leaves removed and stalks trimmed, cut into florets

4 tablespoons butter, divided, plus extra for greasing

½ cup panko bread crumbs

1 tablespoon finely chopped fresh thyme leaves

¼ cup grated Parmesan cheese

3 tablespoons flour

4 cups whole milk

Pinch of ground nutmeg

2 teaspoons Dijon mustard

8 ounces white Cheddar cheese, grated

3 ounces Gruyère cheese, grated

Salt and ground black pepper, to taste

1. Preheat the oven to 375°F.

2. In a large saucepan of boiling salted water, cook the pasta until al dente. Using a slotted spoon, remove the macaroni to a large bowl and set aside.

3. In the same pot of water, add the broccoli florets and cook for 4 to 6 minutes, or until tender. Drain and allow to cool slightly before pureeing in a food processor until smooth.

4. Meanwhile, melt 2 tablespoons of the butter in a large frying pan over medium heat. Add the panko bread crumbs and toast until golden brown. Remove from the heat and stir through the thyme and Parmesan cheese. Set aside.

5. In a large saucepan over medium heat, melt the remaining 2 tablespoons butter. Add the flour, stirring until well combined. Cook out the flour for 2 minutes before gradually whisking in the milk. Over low heat, whisk until thickened, then remove and season with nutmeg. Stir through the mustard, cheeses, and salt and pepper, whisking well to combine. Add the macaroni and fold through the broccoli puree.

6. Butter an 8½-inch x 7½-inch x 3-inch baking dish and tip in the macaroni mixture. Sprinkle over the panko crumb mixture and bake for 25 to 30 minutes, or until golden and bubbling.

MUM'S LASAGNA

My family requests this lasagna for supper all the time, so much so that I usually have a few slices tucked away in the freezer for a quick fix. I like to serve it with a simple green salad and garlic bread. **SERVES 8**

2½ cups whole milk

1 bay leaf

2 medium onions,
   1 finely chopped
   and the other halved

¼ cup butter

¼ cup flour

Salt and ground black
   pepper, to taste

Pinch of ground
   nutmeg

2 tablespoons olive oil

2 cloves garlic, finely
   chopped

1½ pounds good-
   quality lean ground
   beef

2 tablespoons tomato
   paste

1 can (28 ounces)
   good-quality
   chopped tomatoes
   (I like to use San
   Marzano)

½ cup fresh basil
   leaves, roughly
   chopped

½ cup water

1 cup ricotta cheese

1 cup mascarpone
   cheese

Zest of 1 lemon

1. Preheat the oven to 350°F. In a saucepan, combine the milk, bay leaf, and halved onion. Bring to a boil and then remove from the heat and cover with cling film. Allow to infuse for 10 minutes before removing the bay leaf and onion.

2. In a medium saucepan over medium heat, melt the butter. Add the flour and cook for 2 to 3 minutes, stirring constantly until well combined and beginning to bubble. Reduce the heat to low and gradually whisk in the infused milk. Whisk continuously until the mixture begins to thicken. Remove from the heat and set aside to cool slightly. Season with salt, pepper, and nutmeg.

3. In a large saucepan over medium heat, add the olive oil and chopped onion. Cook for 5 minutes, or until beginning to soften. Add the garlic and cook for another 2 minutes, or until fragrant. Add the beef, breaking up the meat with a wooden spoon, and cook for 4 to 6 minutes, or until it begins to turn golden, stirring occasionally. Add the tomato paste and cook for 1 minute before adding the chopped tomatoes, basil, and water. Bring to a boil, reduce the heat, and simmer for 1 hour, uncovered, until thickened and reduced, stirring occasionally. Season to taste with salt and pepper and set aside to cool.

4. In a small bowl, whisk together the ricotta and mascarpone cheeses, season with lemon zest and salt, and set aside.

recipe continues

1 package (16 ounces) lasagna noodles (Buy the dried lasagna sheets that don't need blanching—these are the best!)

12 ounces mozzarella cheese, sliced into rounds

½ cup grated Parmesan cheese

5. In a 9-inch x 12-inch baking dish, begin layering by spreading one-third of the meat sauce on the bottom, followed by dollops of the ricotta mixture, noodles to cover, and then one-half of the white sauce. Repeat another layer and then top with noodles, remaining meat sauce, and mozzarella. Grate ½ cup of Parmesan cheese over the entire dish. Bake for 45 minutes, or until the sauce is bubbling and golden.

TIPS: *The lasagna can be made ahead of time up to the baking step, wrapped in plastic wrap, then foil, and frozen for up to 1 month. To cook from frozen, remove plastic wrap, cover with foil, and bake for 1½ hours before removing the foil and cooking for another 30 minutes, or until bubbling and golden.*

I usually make lasagna to serve to my munchkins, so I leave out the salt. However, if you are making this for a cozy kitchen supper, then add a teaspoon or two of salt to the white sauce. Otherwise, my husband adds a bit of salt to our unsalted kiddie-friendly lasagna and is happy.

PATRICIA'S IRISH STEW

We've been lucky to have a maternity nurse help us following the births of each of our three children. As my family isn't around the corner to lend a hand with a newborn, our nurse Patricia has been an incredible source of support. Along with maintaining some level of sanity in a house with 3 kids under the age of 5, Patricia makes the meanest Irish Stew. I'm always so grateful to have a bowl of Patricia's stew in front of me. **SERVES 4 TO 6**

4 ounces pancetta, diced

1 tablespoon olive oil, plus extra if needed

1 to 1½ pounds boned and diced lamb neck filet or shoulder

Salt and pepper, to taste

2 small onions, chopped

2 leeks, trimmed, cleaned, and sliced

2 cloves garlic, minced

1 tablespoon tomato paste

1 cup red wine

3 medium waxy potatoes, peeled and cubed

3 medium carrots, peeled and cubed

2 medium parsnips, peeled and cubed

½ cup pearl barley

4 cups lamb or Vegetable Stock (page 217)

2 rosemary sprigs

4 thyme sprigs

2 bay leaves

1. Preheat the oven to 300°F and arrange the racks in the middle of the oven.

2. In a heavy-bottomed Dutch oven, sauté the pancetta in the olive oil over medium for 2 to 3 minutes, or until golden. Remove the pancetta with a slotted spoon and set aside.

3. Season the lamb with salt and pepper, and working in batches, sear the meat on all sides until golden, about 2 to 3 minutes. Remove and set aside.

4. Add the onions and leeks to the pan along with a drizzle of oil, if needed, and cook for 4 to 6 minutes, or until softened and beginning to turn golden. Stir often. Add the garlic and cook for 1 minute, then add the tomato paste and cook for 1 minute. Deglaze the pan with the red wine and cook until the wine has been reduced by two-thirds.

5. Add the potatoes, carrots, and parsnips, stirring well to combine, and cook for 3 minutes to gently soften the vegetables. Stir through the barley.

6. Return the lamb and pancetta to the pot and pour the stock over top. Tie the rosemary, thyme, and bay leaves together with kitchen twine, and place them in the stew. Season with salt and pepper.

7. Dampen a piece of parchment paper with water and scrunch it with your hands. Place it on top of the stew and cover with the lid. Place in oven for 1½ hours, stirring halfway, until the lamb is tender and almost falling apart.

WELSH RAREBIT

This is a common British recipe that, if you're not a Brit, sounds a bit strange and is often mistaken for something exotic, when in fact it's simply posh cheese on toast. Spicy and tangy from the mustard and creamy from the egg yolks and cheese, this is toast with serious attitude—one of my major cravings when I was pregnant with our daughter and a treat anytime. Also a *major* hangover helper. Best served with a homemade chutney (page 221). **SERVES 2**

2 egg yolks

1 teaspoon English mustard powder

1 teaspoon Worcestershire sauce

Pinch of cayenne pepper

Salt, to taste

2 thick slices sourdough bread

1 tablespoon butter, softened

2 tablespoons stout

2 cups grated Lancashire cheese or mature Cheddar

1 tablespoon flat-leaf parsley leaves, roughly chopped

1. Preheat the broiler to its highest setting and line a baking tray with aluminum foil. In a small bowl, whisk together the egg yolks, mustard powder, Worcestershire sauce, and cayenne pepper. Season with salt.

2. Place the bread under the broiler and toast for 2 minutes on each side, or until golden.

3. In a bowl, beat together the softened butter and stout with the mustard mixture, and then add the cheese. Pile the mixture onto the toasts and place under the broiler for 3 to 5 minutes, or until golden and bubbling. Allow to cool slightly before garnishing with parsley and serving with Tomato Chutney (page 221) on the side.

LANCASHIRE HOT POT

This is a simple lamb or mutton stew that's best left ticking away in the oven for hours while you go about your day. The key is to keep the flavours simple because they will gain depth and complexity during the slow cooking process. **SERVES 6**

1½ pounds lamb
    shoulder, cut into
    1-inch pieces
Salt and ground black
    pepper, to taste
4 lamb kidneys, cored
    and roughly
    chopped
4 tablespoons flour
6 tablespoons butter,
    divided
2 tablespoons
    sunflower oil
2 onions, thinly sliced
1 carrot, peeled and
    chopped
1 clove garlic, minced
1 bay leaf
Leaves from 2 sprigs
    thyme
Leaves from
    2 rosemary sprigs,
    chopped
2 cups plus
    1½ tablespoons
    lamb stock or
    Chicken Stock
    (page 215)
3–4 large floury
    potatoes, peeled
    and thinly sliced
¼ cup grated Parmesan
    cheese

1. Preheat the oven to 300°F. Toss the lamb shoulder with the flour. Season with salt and pepper and pat off any excess.

2. In a shallow, heavy-bottomed ovenproof casserole dish over medium heat, melt 1 tablespoon butter with 1 tablespoon oil. Brown half of the lamb shoulder, until it begins to turn golden, then remove from the casserole to a bowl. Add another 1 tablespoon each of butter and oil, and brown the second half of the meat; then add it to the bowl.

3. Add 1 tablespoon of butter to the pan and brown the kidneys quickly, then add them to the other lamb.

4. Add the onions to the same casserole along with another tablespoon of butter and stir, cooking for 5 minutes, or until softened. Add the carrot and cook for another few minutes before adding the garlic, bay leaf, thyme, and rosemary, stirring for 1 minute.

5. Add the lamb back into the casserole dish along with the stock. Stir to combine. Cover with a lid and cook the lamb stew on the stovetop for 30 minutes. Remove the lid, and cook for 20 to 30 minutes.

6. Arrange the potato slices in a concentric circle beginning on the outside, slightly overlapping until you reach the centre. Melt the remaining butter and brush it over the potato topping. Sprinkle with Parmesan cheese, salt, and black pepper.

7. Cover and bake for 1 hour, or until the potatoes are tender. Increase the heat to 325°F and bake uncovered for 20 to 30 minutes, or until the potatoes are golden and crisp.

BUBBLE AND SQUEAK

Traditionally, Bubble and Squeak is made with leftover vegetables from a Sunday roast dinner, but our kids love this dish so much that I make it even when we haven't had a big meal the day before. The name comes from the sounds that the potatoes and greens make in the pan while they cook. I like to serve this with roasted sausages and fried eggs for breakfast or a casual weeknight supper. **SERVES 4**

4 tablespoons butter, divided

4 ounces pancetta, chopped

1 red onion, finely chopped

1 leek, cleaned and thinly sliced

1 clove garlic, minced

1 cup shredded kale

Juice from half a lemon

2 cups leftover mashed potatoes

2 tablespoons flat-leaf parsley, finely chopped, plus extra leaves for garnish

Salt and ground black pepper, to taste

4 sausages

4 eggs

TIP: *If you don't have a cast-iron skillet, simply use a good nonstick pan.*

1. Preheat the oven to 100°F. In a 9-inch cast-iron skillet, melt 2 tablespoons of the butter over medium heat. Add the pancetta pieces and cook for 4 to 6 minutes, or until golden. Remove and set aside.

2. Add the red onion and leek to the same pan and cook for 6 to 8 minutes, or until softened and translucent. Add the garlic and cook for another minute or so.

3. Add the pancetta back to the pan along with the kale and cook until the kale is slightly wilted. Remove from the heat and season with lemon juice.

4. Place the mashed potatoes in a large bowl, then add the onion mixture, stirring well to combine. Stir through the parsley and season to taste with salt and pepper.

5. Add the remaining 2 tablespoons butter to the pan and place back over a medium heat to melt. Add the sausages and cook for 3 to 4 minutes, or until crisp. Form the potato mash into 4 patties. Cook for 4 to 6 minutes per side, or until golden and crisp. Place in the oven to keep warm while you prepare the rest.

6. In a separate frying pan over medium heat, cook the eggs for 3 to 4 minutes, or until the whites are set and the edges are crispy.

7. Remove the potato patties and sausages from the oven and carefully tip onto a cutting board. Slice the patties into 4 and top with a sausage and a fried egg. Garnish with extra parsley and a good cracking of black pepper. Serve immediately.

CHAPTER 6

roasts

CLASSIC ROAST BEEF

This is one of the simplest roast meals—perfect for a cozy Sunday lunch with friends and family. Simple recipes are all about the quality of the ingredients—and with roast beef, I like to choose the highest-quality meat that is available. Prime meat has fat marbling throughout the cut, which gives a great flavour. **SERVES 8**

4 banana shallots, peeled and halved

2 red onions, peeled and quartered

3 tablespoons olive oil

Salt and ground black pepper, to taste

3 pounds bone-in rib roast

2 tablespoons English mustard

2 cloves garlic, minced

6 sprigs fresh rosemary, 2 set aside left whole

TIP: *Ask your butcher to truss the roast, which will allow it to cook more evenly (and make it easier to slice).*

1. Preheat the oven to 425°F.

2. In a large bowl, combine the shallots, onions, and 1 tablespoon of olive oil. Toss until well combined and season with salt and pepper.

3. In a separate bowl, combine the mustard, garlic, and remaining olive oil.

4. Season the beef with salt, pepper, and 4 sprigs of rosemary, and place in a large roasting tray. Roast for 20 minutes, then reduce the temperature to 350°F. Baste the meat with the mustard mixture, using the 2 whole rosemary leaves as brushes.

5. Add the onion mixture around the beef and roast for 2 hours, or until the internal temperature reads 145°F to 160°F for medium rare. Baste with the mustard mixture every 20 minutes. Remove and tent with foil to rest. If necessary, return the onion mixture to the oven to cook for another 20 minutes until it is golden and sticky.

6. To serve, slice the beef and serve on top of the sticky onions.

CHILI MINTED PEAS

Mushy peas are synonymous with English cooking. Typically served alongside fish and chips, they are one of those dishes you either love or hate. I like to add a bit of freshness and heat by incorporating mint and chili flakes. The best part about this recipe is that you can use frozen peas, which saves you the time of podding!

When I make mushy peas I always think of my father, who predicted that I would hate British food. "If I wanted my peas mushy, I would chew them myself," he said. My father is right 99 percent of the time, but he underestimated this humble dish. British food is delicious, and I *love* mushy peas. **SERVES 4 TO 6**

1 tablespoon olive oil

1 green onion, finely sliced

2 cups frozen peas

½ teaspoon chili flakes

1 tablespoon fresh lemon juice

3 tablespoons finely shredded fresh mint leaves, divided

Salt and ground black pepper, to taste

1. In a medium saucepan over low heat, add the olive oil and green onion, cooking for 2 minutes, or until the onion begins to soften. Add the peas, chili flakes, and a splash of water. Cover and allow to steam for 3 to 4 minutes, or until vibrant green.

2. Remove the lid and add the lemon juice and 2 tablespoons of the fresh mint. Using a potato masher or a food processor, mash until well combined but still slightly chunky.

3. Season lightly with salt and black pepper, then tip into a bowl and garnish with the remaining 1 tablespoon mint leaves.

STICKY AND SWEET ROASTED CARROTS

Roasting carrots is a great way to pack a lot of flavour into a very simple ingredient. The natural sugars in the carrots caramelize at high heat, yielding deliciously sweet vegetables. **SERVES 4**

1 pound carrots, peeled and halved (tops trimmed and cleaned)
2 tablespoons olive oil
1 tablespoon maple syrup
1 tablespoon cumin seeds
¼ teaspoon cayenne pepper
Salt and ground black pepper, to taste

1. Preheat the oven to 425°F. In a large nonstick baking tray, mix together the carrots, oil, maple syrup, cumin seeds, and cayenne pepper. Season with salt and pepper.

2. Roast for 20 to 30 minutes, depending on the thickness of the carrots, until they are caramelized and tender but still have a bit of bite.

TIPS: *I like to buy carrots with the greens from farmers' markets, as they make for a beautiful presentation on the dinner table.*

If you want a more rustic aesthetic, no need to peel the carrots; just scrub well.

HERB-CRUSTED RACK OF LAMB

A rack of lamb is known as the best end of the lamb—I like to order a "French-trimmed" rack. Though lamb is often served in heavier dishes like pies or stew, a rack is lighter and pairs well with new potatoes and fresh summer vegetables.

SERVES 4 (2 CHOPS EACH)

1 pound rack of lamb, trimmed

2 tablespoons olive oil, divided

Salt and ground black pepper, to taste

1 tablespoon finely chopped rosemary leaves

1 tablespoon finely chopped thyme leaves

2 tablespoons finely chopped flat-leaf parsley leaves

¾ cup fresh bread crumbs

1 tablespoon butter

2 tablespoons Dijon mustard

Minted Yoghurt Sauce (page 137)

1. Preheat the oven to 375°F. Score the fat on the rack of lamb by gently running a knife over it in a criss-cross pattern. With a large piece of tin foil, cover the exposed bones so they don't burn. Rub 1 tablespoon of olive oil into the meat and season with salt and pepper.

2. Heat a large ovenproof pan over medium heat. Add the lamb, scored side down, and cook for 5 minutes or so, or until it becomes golden brown. This seals the meat to keep all the juices in. Meanwhile, combine the remaining 1 tablespoon olive oil, rosemary, thyme, parsley, and bread crumbs in a bowl.

3. Once you have a nice golden colour, add the butter to the pan and carefully, using a spoon, baste the meat with the butter for a minute or so. Place the pan in the oven and roast the rack for 10 minutes. Remove the pan from the oven, and carefully spread the mustard over the golden scored fat. Gently press the herb and bread crumb mixture onto the mustard.

4. Return the rack to the oven and roast for 5 minutes, or until the meat is pink and tender. Allow to rest for 10 minutes before slicing and serving with the Minted Yoghurt Sauce (page 137).

TIP: Rub the rack of lamb with olive oil at least an hour before cooking to allow the oil to soak in and marinate the meat. If you are not going to cook the lamb within 2 hours, refrigerate the rack, then bring it to room temperature an hour before cooking.

ROASTED WINTER VEGETABLES

Though I'm writing this in the middle of July in London, it is cold and rainy, and I've got these supposedly "winter" vegetables in the oven. I couldn't be more excited to dive in. This recipe has less to do with winter itself (naturally, because in England the weather can be dispiriting year-round!) and more with feeling warm and cozy whenever the mood strikes.

Roasting root vegetables brings out their natural sweetness, and I add a fresh herb drizzle to brighten up the flavour. My kids like the drizzle and cheese on the side so they can do the dipping and sprinkling themselves. **SERVES 4 TO 6**

2 fennel bulbs, tops removed

2 small white onions, peeled

1 pound parsnips, peeled

1 pound baby carrots, tops trimmed but kept intact

4 tablespoons olive oil, divided

Salt and ground black pepper, to taste

1 cup finely chopped flat-leaf parsley leaves

Zest and juice from 1 lemon

2 tablespoons grated Parmesan cheese

1. Preheat the oven to 400°F. Line a large baking tray with parchment paper. Cut the fennel bulbs and onions into 6 wedges to keep them intact. Halve and quarter the parsnips and carrots. Place all of the vegetables on the tray and drizzle with 2 tablespoons of the olive oil. Season with salt and pepper and toss to combine. Roast in the oven for 45 to 50 minutes, or until caramelized and tender, tossing halfway.

2. Meanwhile, in a small bowl, combine the remaining 2 tablespoons of olive oil, the parsley, lemon zest, lemon juice, and Parmesan cheese. Season well with salt and pepper.

3. When the vegetables are golden and crisp on the edges, remove from the oven and transfer to a serving platter. Drizzle with the parsley mixture and serve.

YORKSHIRE PUDDING

This side dish is essential to any traditional British roast. Early on in my time in England, I was warned that "Yorkshire Puds" were difficult to pull off, so I felt too intimidated to attempt them. But last Christmas an overwhelming craving struck me, and I thought I might as well *try* (if it's a disaster, I reasoned, they can just be thrown out . . .). Turns out, they were delicious *and* super easy. I've never looked back. **SERVES 8**

¼ cup sunflower oil

1¼ cups all-purpose flour

4 medium eggs, lightly beaten

1 cup plus 2 tablespoons whole milk

2 tablespoons fresh thyme leaves, finely chopped

1 teaspoon salt

1 teaspoon ground black pepper

1. Preheat the oven to 450°F. Divide the oil among the cups of a 12-cup nonstick muffin tin. Place the tin carefully into the oven to preheat.

2. In a large bowl, add the flour and make a well in the centre. Add the eggs and whisk until smooth. Gradually whisk in the milk until the mixture is smooth and fluid. Stir through the thyme, salt, and pepper. Let the batter rest for at least 30 minutes.

3. When ready, remove the hot tin from the oven and carefully pour the batter into the muffin cups, about two-thirds of the way up. Place back into the oven and bake for 18 to 20 minutes, or until puffed and golden brown. Remove and allow to cool slightly before removing from the tin.

TIP: *The baked puddings can be frozen for up to 1 month, then reheated in the oven.*

The secret to Yorkshire pudding is letting the batter rest. Allow 30 minutes minimum or longer if possible.

MINTED YOGHURT SAUCE

My brother-in-law tipped me off about the secret to this sauce: substituting tangy yoghurt for the more traditional cream. It's a great sauce to add to your Sunday roast repertoire, as it works equally well with lamb, chicken, and beef. And since it's a lighter option than cream sauce, you will have more room for Sticky Toffee Pudding (page 202). **SERVES 6**

1½ cups plain yoghurt

1 shallot, very finely chopped

1 teaspoon ground cumin

1 tablespoon fresh mint leaves, finely chopped

1 tablespoon fresh coriander leaves, finely chopped

1 tablespoon lemon zest

2 tablespoons lemon juice

Salt and ground black pepper, to taste

In a bowl, mix together the yoghurt, shallot, cumin, mint, coriander, lemon zest, and lemon juice. Season with salt and pepper and serve alongside the Herb-Crusted Rack of Lamb (page 132).

***

TIPS: *You can make the sauce a day in advance. Substitute any fresh herb if there is something you prefer.*

BREAD SAUCE

This is a very traditional British side dish, especially at Christmas, and it goes well with any roast. It may sound a bit odd, but it is unbelievably satisfying when eaten with juicy meat and vegetables. I like to make my own sourdough bread crumbs from leftover bread I've got lying around by simply leaving the torn bread out to dry overnight then blitzing in a food processor until fine. **SERVES 6**

2 cups whole milk

2 tablespoons unsalted butter

1 clove garlic, minced

4 cloves

½ cinnamon stick

1 bay leaf

2 sprigs fresh thyme

1 sprig fresh rosemary

1 cup sourdough bread crumbs (or use fresh store bought)

¼ cup mascarpone

Salt and ground black pepper, to taste

1. In a saucepan over medium heat, combine the milk, butter, garlic, cloves, cinnamon, bay leaf, thyme, and rosemary. Simmer over very low heat for 20 minutes to infuse the flavours.

2. Strain the milk mixture through a fine sieve into a clean pan and place back over medium heat. Add the bread crumbs and stir, cooking for 5 minutes, or until slightly thickened. Remove from the heat and stir through the mascarpone. Season with salt and pepper and serve.

TIP: *This can be made up to 3 days in advance, stored in the fridge in an airtight container, and reheated gently over the stove.*

PERFECT ROAST CHICKEN

The key to a delicious roast chicken is to brine it—or, as my kids call it—"put the chicken in a bath." It's a simple technique, but remember that brining a chicken takes 18 hours and then it needs to dry and rest uncovered in the refrigerator for 12 more hours, so it is necessary to start the process 2 days before you plan on having roast chicken for supper. The preparation is well worth it, though; brining tenderizes the meat, locks in the moisture, crisps the skin, and makes the bird completely irresistible. **SERVES 4**

A Day Ahead: Brine
½ cup sugar
½ cup kosher salt
6 cups water
4 bay leaves
2 tablespoons peppercorns
1 chicken (3 pounds)

1. *To make the brine:* Place the sugar, salt, water, bay leaves, and peppercorns in a medium saucepan, bring to a boil, and cook until the sugar and salt have dissolved. Allow to cool completely—or if you are in a rush, add ice to make the water room temperature.

2. Place the chicken in a large bowl or pot and pour the cooled brine mixture over the top to cover it completely. Add more water if necessary to cover the chicken. You can put a plate on top of the pot to keep the chicken submerged. Refrigerate for 18 hours.

3. Remove the chicken and pat dry with paper towels, then put back in refrigerator on a plate and let air dry, uncovered, for another 12 hours.

Roast the Chicken

2 onions, peeled and quartered

2 shallots, peeled and halved

1 lemon, cut into wedges

2 sprigs fresh thyme

2 tablespoons olive oil, divided

Salt and ground black pepper, to taste

¼ cup butter, softened

4. *To roast the chicken:* Remove the chicken from the refrigerator an hour before roasting so that it can warm to room temperature. Preheat the oven to 400°F. In a large roasting tray, place the onions, shallots, lemon, and thyme sprigs. Toss with 1 tablespoon of the olive oil and season well with salt and pepper.

5. Rub the butter underneath the chicken skin. Season the chicken with the remaining 1 tablespoon olive oil and pepper to taste—you do not need to add more salt to a chicken that has already been brined. Tie the legs together with kitchen twine.

6. Place the chicken on top of the onions, and roast in the oven for 1 hour, basting occasionally. The chicken is cooked if the juices run clear when piercing the thickest part of the meat. If not, return the chicken to the oven, and check again after a few minutes.

7. Let the chicken rest for 20 minutes. This is really important, as the chicken continues to cook. Turn the chicken over on its back (this is a trick my mother-in-law taught me—it allows the juices to run through the chicken) and cover with aluminum foil while it is resting.

BUTTERNUT SQUASH MASH

Butternut squash is in the paleo diet (✔), has a low GI (✔), tastes wonderful, *and* is a nice change from regular mash. My kids prefer it because of the sweeter flavour, and it is even more delicious with the addition of orange zest. **SERVES 6**

2 butternut squash, halved and seeds removed

2 tablespoons olive oil

Salt and ground black pepper, to taste

2 tablespoons butter

Zest from 1 orange

1. Preheat the oven to 400°F. Place the squash halves cut side up on a baking tray. Drizzle with the olive oil and season with a pinch of salt and pepper.

2. Roast for 40 to 50 minutes, or until tender. Remove and allow to cool slightly.

3. Scoop out the flesh and place in a food processor along with the butter and some orange zest. Puree until smooth, season to taste, and garnish with the remaining zest.

TIPS: *Roasting the squash as opposed to steaming it brings out the natural sugars and flavour.*

You can add 1 tablespoon of maple syrup along with the olive oil for extra sweetness.

BRAISED SAVOY CABBAGE

We are a cabbage family—coleslaw when the sun is shining and braised savoy cabbage when we want to cozy up. Cabbage now rules Christmas, too. For years I made Brussels sprouts, but now I make this Braised Savoy Cabbage on Christmas Day (and several other winter evenings, too). **SERVES 6**

2 tablespoons butter

4 ounces pancetta, cut into thin lardoons

4 spring onions, thinly sliced

1 clove garlic, minced

1 Savoy cabbage, outer leaves removed, cut into 8 wedges

½ cup dried bread crumbs

Leaves from 2 thyme sprigs

1 tablespoon grated Parmesan cheese

⅔ cup Chicken Stock (page 215) or Vegetable Stock (page 217)

1. Preheat the oven to 425°F. In an ovenproof frying pan over medium heat, melt the butter. Add the pancetta and cook for 4 to 6 minutes, or until golden and crisp. Using a slotted spoon, transfer the pancetta to a small bowl and set aside.

2. Add the onions and garlic to the pan and cook for 7 minutes, or until softened and golden. Add the cabbage, cut sides down, and cook for 3 minutes per side, or until crisp and golden.

3. Meanwhile, add the bread crumbs, thyme, and cheese to the bowl with the pancetta and stir to combine.

4. Add the stock to the skillet and cook for 2 minutes, turning the cabbage wedges. Sprinkle the bread crumb mixture over the top and bake in the oven for 10 minutes, or until the bread crumbs are golden and the cabbage is tender.

CAULIFLOWER CHEESE

I make cauliflower cheese at least once a week; my husband loves it with his Sunday roast, and the kids often eat it for lunch or supper. I had never had cauliflower cheese until I moved to England, so now I'm ready to have this comforting dish anytime, anywhere—I need to make up for lost time!

There are so many variations of this recipe—you can substitute different cheeses, use more or less depending on how cheesy you want your dish, use a bit of double cream rather than the full quantity of milk, use Dijon rather than mustard powder . . . it is totally up to you. The one thing I always do, and will recommend, is to make more than you think you need. Everyone *always* goes back for seconds. **SERVES 6**

2 heads cauliflower or Romanesco broccoli (see Tip)
¼ cup butter
1 clove garlic, thinly sliced
¼ cup flour
2 cups whole milk
1 teaspoon mustard powder
1 teaspoon cayenne pepper
Salt and ground black pepper, to taste
2 cups grated mature white Cheddar cheese
2 tablespoons fresh flat-leaf parsley leaves, chopped finely

1. Preheat the oven to 375°F. In a large saucepan of boiling water, blanch the cauliflower for 4 minutes. Remove and let cool. Break into florets and set aside.

2. In a small saucepan, melt the butter with the garlic. Add the flour, and using a wooden spoon, mix well until combined. Cook the flour mixture for 2 minutes before gradually adding the milk, whisking to combine. Add the mustard powder and cayenne pepper and cook over low heat, stirring constantly, until thickened. Season with salt and pepper. Remove from the heat and add the cheese.

3. Mix together the cauliflower and cheese mixture. Place in a 13-inch by 9-inch ovenproof dish and bake for 30 minutes, or until golden and bubbly. Garnish with parsley and serve.

TIP: *If you can find Romanesco broccoli, use it. It adds a nutty flavour to the dish.*

ROAST WHOLE SEA BASS

A lot of people find whole fish intimidating to cook, when in fact it's one of the simplest dishes to prepare if you get your fishmonger to do the hard work for you. Buy a cleaned, gutted, and scaled fish, and you're practically ready to go. Make sure the eyes of the fish are clear and the smell is of the sea—that's the best indication of a fresh fish. Roasting it in the oven to perfection and serving it alongside Jersey Royals with Salsa Verde (page 148) makes for the perfect summer meal. I prefer to cook round fish and stuff the cavity with fragrant lemon and fresh herbs. **SERVES 4**

2 tablespoons olive oil, divided, plus additional to serve

4 whole sea bass, cleaned and scaled

1 lemon, sliced

2 cloves garlic, thinly sliced

1 small bunch parsley, plus additional finely chopped to serve

1 small bunch rosemary

Sea salt and ground black pepper, to taste

1. Preheat the oven to 400°F and position a rack in the middle of the oven. Lightly grease a large baking tray with 1 tablespoon of the olive oil.

2. Gently wash the inside cavity of the fish and pat dry with a paper towel. Lay the lemon slices and garlic inside the fish, along with the parsley and rosemary. Season with a pinch of sea salt.

3. Rub the outside of the fish with the remaining 1 tablespoon olive oil. Season well with sea salt and pepper. Using a sharp knife, make 3 or 4 light ¾-inch-long incisions on an angle across the body of each fish; when they bake, these incisions will open and crisp up.

4. Place the fish on the baking tray. Roast for 15 to 20 minutes, or until the flesh is opaque and the skin is just starting to split.

5. Gently remove the fillets from the bone and serve with a drizzle of olive oil and a sprinkling of parsley leaves.

JERSEY ROYALS WITH SALSA VERDE

I grew up on classic tomato-based salsa, but my mother-in-law taught me this version, and my husband loves the caper and anchovy flavours. I usually use it as a dip for tortilla chips, but it also adds pizzazz to meat, fish, or roasted vegetables—just drizzle on top. **SERVES 4**

1½ pounds Jersey Royals or a waxy potato

½ cup chives, finely chopped

½ cup basil, finely chopped

¼ cup flat-leaf parsley, finely chopped

¼ cup dill, finely chopped

1 clove garlic, finely chopped

1 teaspoon Dijon mustard

2 teaspoons capers

2 anchovies, finely chopped

1 red chili, deseeded and finely chopped (optional)

1 tablespoon red wine vinegar

½ cup olive oil

Salt and ground black pepper

1. In a large saucepan, cook the potatoes in salted boiling water for 13 minutes, or until cooked through and fork tender but not falling apart. Drain and allow to steam dry.

2. In a small bowl, combine the chives, basil, parsley, dill, garlic, mustard, capers, anchovies, chili, and vinegar. Gradually whisk in the olive oil, and season well with the salt and pepper.

3. Delicately dress the potatoes with the dressing so they are completely covered and well combined. Serve warm or at room temperature.

DAUPHINOISE POTATOES

My rule of thumb is everything in moderation, including these decadent potatoes. I believe if you're going to enjoy something rich and creamy, it may as well be delicious. I'll serve these at any holiday gathering. I add a twist to the traditional classic French comfort food by adding caramelized fennel and onion. **SERVES 6**

2 tablespoons butter, divided

1 fennel bulb, cored and thinly sliced

1 small onion, thinly sliced

2 cloves garlic, thinly sliced

Sea salt, to taste

2 pounds floury potatoes, peeled and very thinly sliced

1¼ cups heavy cream

¾ cup plus 1 tablespoon whole milk

½ teaspoon ground nutmeg

Ground black pepper, to taste

½ cup grated Parmesan cheese

1. Preheat the oven to 350°F. Grease an 11-inch x 7-inch ovenproof baking dish with 1 tablespoon of the butter.

2. In a large skillet over medium heat, melt the remaining 1 tablespoon butter. Add the fennel, onion, and garlic and cook for 15 to 20 minutes, or until softened, golden, and caramelized. Season with a pinch of salt and remove from the heat to cool slightly.

3. Layer the potatoes in rows in the baking dish, ensuring that they overlap slightly. After your first layer, add one-quarter of the fennel and onion mixture. Repeat with the remaining potatoes and fennel and onion mixture, finishing with the potatoes.

4. In a large bowl, mix together the cream, milk, and nutmeg. Season with sea salt and pepper. Pour evenly on top of the potatoes, then gently press the potatoes down with a flat spatula so they begin to submerge in the cream mixture.

5. Sprinkle the cheese on top of the mixture and cover with foil. Bake for 40 to 45 minutes, or until the potatoes are almost tender. Remove the foil and bake for 15 minutes, or until golden and bubbly.

party picks

PFG (PEA-FETA GUACAMOLE)

This dip is a Hermer household staple. It is easy to whip up when friends stop by, and my munchkins love dipping their crudités in a bowl of PFG while I finish making their supper. **SERVES 4 TO 6**

½ cup peas, fresh
    or frozen

3 ripe avocados,
    halved, pits
    removed

½ cup diced feta cheese

1 chili, chopped

⅓ cup chopped mint

Juice from 2–3 limes

Salt and ground black
    pepper, to taste

1 jalapeño pepper,
    thinly sliced

1. Bring a small pot of water to a boil. Add the peas and cook for 1 minute. Drain and place in a bowl of ice water or run under cold water until completely cool. Drain on paper towels.

2. Place the avocados, feta cheese, chili, mint, lime juice, and peas in a food processor or a blender. Blend until creamy. Season to taste with salt and pepper, and scatter jalapeño over the top.

3. Serve with tortilla chips, crackers, or veggies.

TIP: *The lime juice keeps this dip from turning brown so you can make it in advance of your party or the night before.*

BAKED CHEESE

A lovely warm and gooey baked cheese will always be a winner. My favourite cheese is Mont d'Or, a raw milk cheese that turns ultra-smooth and velvety when baked. If you can't find that variety, substitute an equally delicious Camembert or Brie.

SERVES 4 TO 6

1 **Vacherin Mont d'Or or Camembert cheese, at room temperature**

1 **clove garlic, thinly sliced**

2 **rosemary sprigs, cut into thirds**

1 **tablespoon olive oil**

1 **teaspoon chili flakes (optional)**

1. Preheat the oven to 400°F. Remove the cheese from the container and place on a baking tray lined with parchment paper.

2. With a sharp knife, gently make 3 incisions in the top of the cheese. Stuff the sliced garlic into the incisions. Carefully add the rosemary sprigs into the incisions as well.

3. Drizzle the cheese with the olive oil, sprinkle with the chili flakes (if using), and bake for 10 minutes, or until it's oozing and melting. Serve immediately.

HUMMUS

I always have a pot of homemade hummus in the fridge. The kids love it with their carrots and cucumbers, and I always find myself adding it to pieces of chicken or sliced turkey for a quick pick-me-up.

There are many tricks to making a good hummus, and everyone has an opinion when it comes to this ubiquitous dip. You can easily adapt the flavours to your preferences. I love adding cooked beetroot for a sweeter, more vibrant dip, or adding fresh herbs like coriander. **SERVES 4**

1 can (15½ ounces) chickpeas, rinsed and drained

3 cloves garlic, peeled

¼ cup tahini paste

3 tablespoons lemon juice

1 teaspoon ground cumin

1 teaspoon sea salt, to taste

6 tablespoons olive oil, plus extra to drizzle

1 tablespoon toasted sesame seeds

1 teaspoon sweet smoked paprika

1. Place the chickpeas and garlic in the food processor and pulse until roughly chopped and broken down. While the motor is running, add the tahini paste, lemon juice, and cumin. Keep the motor running for 5 minutes, or until the hummus is smooth and creamy. Add the salt to taste.

2. Place in a bowl and, using the back of a spoon, make a slight but shallow indent in the centre. Drizzle with olive oil and sprinkle over the sesame seeds and paprika.

SPICED NUT MIX

There is something so satisfying and addictive about the sweet-and-salty combination of these mixed nuts. They're perfect to snack on with a glass of wine or to have around the house when guests drop by unannounced. This recipe makes a large amount; the mix can be stored in an airtight container in the refrigerator for up to 2 weeks. **SERVES 4 TO 6**

2 cups almonds, skins on

1 cup walnut halves

1 cup pecan halves

1 cup cashews

¼ cup pumpkin seeds

2 tablespoons sesame seeds

3 tablespoons olive oil

3 tablespoons maple syrup

1 teaspoon smoked paprika

1 teaspoon cayenne pepper

Leaves from 2 sprigs rosemary, very finely chopped

1 teaspoon sea salt

1. Preheat the oven to 325°F. Line a baking tray with parchment paper.

2. In a large bowl, combine the nuts, seeds, olive oil, maple syrup, paprika, cayenne, rosemary leaves, and sea salt. Stir well.

3. Tip onto the baking tray and bake for 20 to 25 minutes, or until golden brown and sticky. Allow to cool completely.

TAPENADE

One of the easiest snacks to make—all you need is a food processor. **SERVES 4 TO 6**

1 cup pitted kalamata
    olives

½ cup pitted green
    Nocellara olives (or
    other green variety)

¼ cup sun-dried
    tomatoes packed
    in oil, roughly
    chopped

1 teaspoon sugar

1 tablespoon fresh
    flat-leaf parsley,
    roughly chopped

Pinch of ground black
    pepper

⅓ cup good-quality
    olive oil plus
    additional if
    needed

1. In a food processor, combine the olives and tomatoes. Pulse a couple of times to roughly chop. Add the sugar and parsley, pulsing again until the mixture is coarsely ground.

2. Add the pepper and ⅓ cup olive oil. Pulse again until the mixture becomes smoother but still has a few chunky pieces. Add a bit more olive oil if necessary.

TIPS: *This tapenade will keep up to 1 week in an airtight container in the refrigerator.*

Nocellara olives are large green olives that originate from Sicily and are used both as eating and olive oil production olives. They are slightly sweet with a mild buttery flavour and texture.

CORIANDER COBBLER

This refreshing cocktail is perfect for an outdoor BBQ or an afternoon lunch in warmer weather. Be careful, though—they go down easy! **SERVES 1**

Coriander Syrup
3½ ounces coriander
1 bottle Monin or Teisseire gomme syrup

Coriander Cobbler
4 slices cucumber
1 ounce Hendrick's Gin
½ ounce lemon juice
¾ ounce Coriander Syrup
1 ounce dry white wine
Cucumber, for garnish

1. *To make the coriander syrup:* Add the coriander to the bottle of gomme syrup. Let infuse for 24 hours, then remove the coriander from the bottle.

2. *To make the coriander cobbler:* Muddle the cucumber slices in a cocktail shaker. Pour the gin, lemon juice, coriander syrup, and wine into the shaker. Shake and strain into a wineglass filled with ice cubes.

3. Peel a slice of cucumber with a peeler and place it around the glass as a garnish.

TIP: *Premake the cucumber peels and leave in ice water until ready to serve.*

ECLIPSE'S WATERMELON MARTINI

On my first date with my now-husband, we went to his bar Eclipse on Walton Street, and he ordered me a watermelon martini. I'll never know if it was this drink that sealed it or if I had already fallen for the man, but after a couple of these, I was sold!

SERVES 1

Kaffir Syrup
1 bottle Monin or Teisseire gomme syrup
8–10 kaffir lime leaves

Martini
1 chunk watermelon (the size of 2 big fists)
2 ounces vodka for highball or 1½ ounces for martini glass
¾ ounce kaffir-infused gomme syrup or ½ ounce for martini glass
1 slice watermelon, for garnish

1. *To make the kaffir syrup:* Infuse the bottle of gomme with the kaffir lime leaves and leave for a week.

2. *To make the martini:* Cut the watermelon into a cocktail shaker. Pour the vodka and kaffir syrup at the same time into the glass and shake hard.

3. Single strain into a highball glass or double strain for a martini glass. Add garnish on top.

DARK ECLIPSE

This is one of our signature cocktails at our Eclipse bars in London, Barcelona, and Istanbul. I love the freshness of the berries with the citrus. **SERVES 1**

1 small chunk (fist size) watermelon

6 blackberries

1 tablespoon caster sugar (superfine sugar)

4 teaspoons fresh lime juice

1½ ounces vodka

2 teaspoons crème de mure (available in specialty liqueur shops) or other blackberry liqueur

1. Cut the watermelon chunk into small pieces and place in a cocktail shaker.

2. Add the blackberries, sugar, lime juice, vodka, and crème de mure. Shake well. Pour into a highball glass over ice.

BUMPKIN'S ENGLISH GARDEN

We know the Queen loves gin, so I always feel properly patriotic when I drink this summer cocktail. **SERVES 1**

1½ ounces gin

1½ ounces apple juice

4 teaspoons elderflower cordial

Juice from half a lemon

3 slices cucumber

5 mint leaves

1. In a cocktail shaker, combine the gin, apple juice, elderflower cordial, lemon juice, cucumber, and mint. Shake well.

2. Pour into a glass filled with ice and serve.

TOTAL ECLIPSE

At Middlebury College, my alma mater, we would make lethal party punch that started with a couple of handles of cheap vodka and ended with an unforgiving hangover. The Total Eclipse is the grown-up version of that poisonous college potion. This is much prettier and significantly better tasting, but still packs a punch. **SERVES A CROWD**

1 whole watermelon
15 ounces vodka
5 ounces Kaffir Syrup (page 163)
Long straws (19 inches is ideal)
Prosecco

1. Place ice (if possible, crushed ice) into a bowl (ideally wooden). Place the watermelon in the middle of the bowl.

2. Cut off the top of the watermelon to make a lid and then, using an apple corer, cut 4 holes in the lid for the straws.

3. Scoop the inside of the watermelon into 4 cocktail shakers. Pour the vodka and Kaffir Syrup at the same time into the shakers. Shake hard and double strain back into the watermelon.

4. Place the lid with 4 holes on the top of the watermelon. Add some crushed ice inside the watermelon to keep it cold. Place long straws in the holes, and fill the watermelon to the top with prosecco.

PIMM'S CUP

When the summer sun hits London, Brits head to their local pub for their first Pimm's Cup of the season. It's a thirst-quenching, summery drink that mixes lemon-lime soda (Sprite or 7UP) with cucumber, mint, fruit, and some Pimm's No. 1, a gin drink that's available at any liquor store. We serve Pimm's Cups at our Eclipse bars and Bumpkin restaurants, and it is a must for Wimbledon tennis, cricket matches, or garden parties. **SERVES 4**

2 oranges, sliced and cut into half-moons

2 lemons, sliced and cut into half-moons

1 Persian cucumber (or a 3-inch-long piece of English cucumber), sliced

2 cups Pimm's No. 1

4 cups Sprite, 7UP, or other lemon-lime soda

6–8 sprigs mint (crushed gently)

1. Fill 2 pitchers one-quarter full with ice.

2. Place a layer of orange slices, lemon slices, and cucumber slices over the ice in each pitcher.

3. Repeat until you get three-quarters of the way to the top of the pitchers.

4. Pour in the Pimm's and the soda, dividing equally between the pitchers, and mix with a spoon.

5. Divide the mint among the pitchers. Be sure to include a few cucumber and fruit slices when you pour each serving.

PARTY STARTER

My husband started serving this shot at Eclipse on Walton Street more than 15 years ago, we served it at our wedding, and for any real party at home I love to surprise our guests with one upon arrival. It does just what it says it is going to do! **MAKES 1 SHOT**

½ ounce vodka

½ ounce passionfruit puree

1 teaspoon gomme syrup

1 teaspoon Chambord

1 tablespoon plus 1 teaspoon prosecco

1. Pour the vodka, passionfruit puree, gomme, and Chambord into a cocktail shaker.

2. Shake and double strain into a double shot glass. Top up with prosecco.

tea time

CUCUMBER SMOKED SALMON SANDWICHES WITH HERBY CREAM CHEESE

This is elegant finger food, perfect for serving with afternoon tea. When I met my mother-in-law, Gloria, for the first time, she served Matt and me these sandwiches at her house. I ate them all and then spent the rest of our visit feeling slightly embarrassed about stuffing my face—I'm not sure I even looked up while I was shovelling them down.

The sandwiches can be made a couple hours ahead and stored in the refrigerator until ready to eat. Lightly spritz the sandwiches with water to prevent them from going dry if you're making them ahead of time. **MAKES 16 FINGER SANDWICHES, SERVES 2 TO 4**

8 ounces cream cheese, at room temperature

1 shallot, finely chopped

1 tablespoon finely chopped fresh dill

1 tablespoon finely chopped fresh chives

Zest and juice from 1 lemon

Salt and ground black pepper, to taste

8 slices whole meal or plain soft bread

½ cucumber, very thinly sliced

4 ounces smoked salmon

1 tablespoon butter

1. In a small bowl, whip together the cream cheese, shallot, dill, chives, lemon zest, and lemon juice. Season with salt and pepper.

2. Spread the cream cheese mixture evenly onto 4 slices of bread. Top with cucumber slices, slightly overlapping, then a couple pieces of smoked salmon.

3. Lightly butter the other 4 slices of bread, then place on top of the ones with the salmon filling. Trim the edges and discard. Cut each into 4 even fingers.

CORONATION CHICKEN SANDWICHES

My kids love little tea sandwiches, which are just the right size for tots. I often pack their school lunches with coronation chicken sandwiches made from leftover roast chicken. These also make a delicious party snack if you scoop the chicken mixture onto baby gem lettuce leaves for bite-size morsels minus the bread. If you really want to be decadent (and why not?), switch the bread for croissants.

MAKES 16 FINGER SANDWICHES, SERVES 2 TO 4

3 chicken breasts, cooked and shredded

4 dried apricots, finely chopped

1 tablespoon curry powder

1 teaspoon ground ginger

1 tablespoon mango chutney

¼ cup mayonnaise

¼ cup plain yoghurt

1 tablespoon finely chopped fresh coriander

Salt and ground black pepper, to taste

8 slices whole meal or plain bread

4 leaves baby romaine lettuce

1. In a large bowl, combine the chicken, apricots, curry, ginger, chutney, mayonnaise, yoghurt, and coriander and mix well. Season with salt and pepper.

2. Divide the chicken mixture onto 4 slices of bread. Top with the lettuce and the remaining bread slices. Trim the edges, then cut each into 4 fingers.

FYI: *Developed by the founder of Le Cordon Bleu cooking school, coronation chicken salad was prepared by the school's students for the queen's coronation in 1953.*

WELSH CAKES

My husband was born and raised in Cardiff, the capital of Wales. We were all told that the way to a man's heart is through his stomach, so when I was dating Matt, I quickly learned how to make *Pice ar y maen*, or Welsh cakes. These teatime treats are cooked in a cast-iron skillet, which gives them a crisp edge and a soft, fluffy centre. Once you've mastered the basic cake, you can easily make variations like the savoury leek and cheese version on page 178. **MAKES 20**

2 cups self-rising flour

¼ cup granulated sugar

1 teaspoon ground cinnamon

½ teaspoon ground nutmeg

¼ teaspoon ground allspice

1 cup butter, chilled and cut into cubes, plus extra for the pan

¾ cup raisins or sultanas

1 teaspoon salt

1 large egg, lightly beaten

1–2 tablespoons milk

1. Sieve the flour into a large bowl. Add the sugar, cinnamon, nutmeg, and allspice, stirring to combine.

2. Add the butter and, with your fingers, begin to crumble and rub the butter and flour mixture together until it resembles fine crumbs. Add the dried fruit and salt, then pour in the beaten egg with 1 tablespoon of milk. Use a fork to bring the mixture together, adding more milk if needed. The mixture should be soft, not sticky. Be careful not to work it too much.

3. Gather the dough into a ball and allow to rest for 5 minutes under a tea towel while you clear a surface.

4. Place a large cast-iron skillet over low-medium heat. The key here is to control the temperature.

5. On a lightly floured surface, roll out the dough until it's about ¼ inch thick. Cut 1½- to 2-inch rounds and set aside while you reroll the remaining dough to stamp out more shapes.

6. Add butter to the pan, swirling to coat. Add the cakes and cook for 4 minutes per side, or until golden and puffed up.

7. Allow to cool slightly, then slice in half and serve with butter, clotted cream, or lightly whipped cream.

LEEK AND CHEESE WELSH CAKES

The classic Welsh cake is sweet, but I prefer this savoury version, perfect for a late afternoon snack. **MAKES 20**

1 tablespoon olive oil

1 leek, trimmed and cleaned, thinly sliced

1 clove garlic, minced

Salt and ground black pepper, to taste

2 cups self-rising flour

1 tablespoon granulated sugar

¼ teaspoon ground nutmeg

1 cup butter, chilled and cut into cubes, plus extra for the pan

½ cup finely grated Cheddar cheese

1 large egg, lightly beaten

1–2 tablespoons milk

1. In a large, nonstick frying pan over medium heat, cook the olive oil and leek for 10 minutes, adding the garlic halfway through, until soft and slightly golden. Remove and allow to cool completely. Season with salt and pepper.

2. Sieve the flour into a large bowl. Add the sugar and nutmeg, stirring to combine.

3. Add the butter and with your fingers, begin to crumble and rub the butter and flour mixture together until it resembles fine crumbs. Add the cooled leek mixture, cheese, and 1 teaspoon salt, then pour in the beaten egg with 1 tablespoon of milk. Use a fork to bring the mixture together, adding more milk if needed. The mixture should be soft, not sticky. Be careful not to work it too much.

4. Gather the dough into a ball and allow to rest for 5 minutes under a tea towel while you clear a surface.

5. Place a large, cast-iron skillet over low-medium heat. The key here is to control the temperature.

6. On a lightly floured surface, roll out the dough until it's about ¼ inch thick. Cut 1½- to 2-inch rounds and set aside while you reroll the remaining dough to stamp out more shapes.

7. Add butter to the pan, swirling to coat. Add the cakes and cook for 4 minutes per side, or until golden and puffed up.

8. Allow to cool slightly, then slice in half and serve with butter.

EGG SALAD SANDWICHES

It was a spring Sunday, and Matt wanted to take me for a picnic in Hyde Park before driving me to the airport to fly back to New York. He led me to a little corner sandwich shop in South Kensington and ordered us 2 egg salad sandwiches and a couple bags of sea salt and vinegar crisps (aka chips). We took our brown bags into the park and stretched out on a bench next to the Serpentine. It was there, while we were eating our sandwiches, that he asked if I would move to London to live with him. I told him he was completely crazy and that it would never work. I also said yes. (PS: It worked.)

I grew up loving egg salad sandwiches—my mother would make them for my school lunch—and now I love them even more. Some couples plan their futures over champagne—for Matt and me, it was egg salad.

Any traditional tea sandwich platter includes egg salad sandwiches. I put mine together with yoghurt to cut down on the mayonnaise and make them a bit healthier.

MAKES 16 FINGER SANDWICHES, SERVES 2 TO 4

6 large eggs
¼ cup good-quality mayonnaise
¼ cup plain yoghurt
1 tablespoon finely chopped fresh dill
1 teaspoon Dijon mustard
4 cornichons, finely chopped
4 radishes, finely chopped
Salt and ground black pepper, to taste
8 slices whole grain or plain bread
4 radishes, thinly sliced

1. Bring a large pot of water to a boil over high heat. Once boiling, reduce the heat to a soft boil and carefully add the eggs. Cook for 10 minutes. With a slotted spoon, gently remove the eggs and place in a large bowl of ice water to chill completely.

2. Remove the shells from the eggs and discard. Roughly chop the eggs and add to a large bowl along with the mayonnaise, yoghurt, dill, mustard, cornichons, and chopped radishes. Season with salt and pepper.

3. Divide the mix among 4 slices of bread and top with the thinly sliced radishes, slightly overlapping. Place the remaining bread slices on top. Trim the edges of the bread and discard. Cut each into 4 even fingers.

TIP: *I like to add cornichons and radishes to my mix, but you can also add chopped red bell peppers and celery, depending on how crunchy you want your egg spread.*

STRAWBERRY SHORTCAKE CUPCAKES

This is my take on a strawberry Victoria sponge, one of England's most famed cakes. These cupcakes are simple to make ahead and great for kids to decorate. Delicious lemon sponge topped with freshly whipped strawberry icing and strawberries—it tastes like English summer at its finest. **MAKES 12 CUPCAKES**

1 cup butter, softened

1¼ cups granulated sugar

4 large eggs

2 cups all-purpose flour

2 teaspoons baking powder

1 teaspoon vanilla extract

Zest from ½ lemon

½ cup strawberries, hulled, plus 12 small strawberries for garnish

1 cup cream cheese

1 cup mascarpone, softened

Seeds from ½ vanilla pod

1½ cups icing sugar, sifted

1. Preheat the oven to 350°F. Line a 12-hole muffin tray with paper cups.

2. In an electric mixer fitted with a paddle attachment, combine the butter and granulated sugar and beat for 4 minutes, or until light and fluffy. Gradually add the eggs, one by one, mixing in between. If the mixture begins to look curdled, add a couple tablespoons of flour. Add the remaining flour, baking powder, vanilla, and lemon zest, folding to combine.

3. Place the mixture into a piping bag and fill the cups two-thirds of the way. Bake for 20 to 22 minutes, or until puffed and golden. Remove and allow to cool completely.

4. Meanwhile, place ½ cup of strawberries in a food processor and pulse until smooth. Pass through a sieve.

5. In a large bowl, whisk the cream cheese until soft and smooth. Add the mascarpone and continue to whisk, then add the vanilla seeds until thoroughly combined. Gradually add the icing sugar until the mixture begins to thicken and it is smooth and shiny but still holds its shape. Fold through the strawberry puree. Place the mix into a piping bag fitted with a star nozzle and refrigerate until ready to use. Quarter the remaining strawberries for garnish.

6. To assemble, pipe a swirl of icing onto the cupcakes and garnish with strawberry pieces.

SCONES

The quintessential English teatime treat, scones are best served straight from the oven, spread generously with clotted cream and jam. The addition of cream to the dough itself makes these scones particularly rich and decadent. I always make sure to have a batch in the oven when friends from out of town come to visit, as nothing is more British than a scone, and the buttery scent they give off while baking revives the weariest of travelers. **MAKES 12**

2½ cups all-purpose flour
2½ teaspoons baking powder
1 teaspoon salt
¼ cup granulated sugar, divided
½ cup butter, chilled and cut into cubes
3 large eggs
1 tablespoon water
⅓ cup plus 1½ tablespoons heavy cream

1. Preheat the oven to 375°F. Line a large baking tray with parchment paper. In a large bowl, sift together the flour, baking powder, and salt. Add 1 tablespoon of the sugar and stir to combine.

2. Add the butter cubes and, using your fingers, quickly rub the butter into the flour mixture until it forms small crumbs. Gradually add the cream and 2 eggs, and use a fork to help combine the mix. It should be soft but not sticky. If needed, sprinkle in a little extra flour. Form the mixture into a ball of dough and allow to rest for 5 minutes.

3. On a lightly floured surface, roll out the dough to 1½ inches thick. Using a 1½- to 2-inch fluted cutter, stamp out scones and place them on the lined tray.

4. Lightly brush the scones with an egg wash made from the remaining egg beaten with the water. Sprinkle with the remaining 1 tablespoon sugar.

5. Bake for 12 to 14 minutes, or until puffed and golden brown. Allow to cool slightly before serving with jam and clotted cream.

TIP: *Make sure to not work the dough too much. Quickly bringing it together and allowing it to rest will relax the gluten and yield lighter, fluffier scones.*

CHEDDAR AND CHIVE SCONES

This is a simple way to create a savoury version of the classic recipe. I like to serve them topped with avocado mash and a fried egg for breakfast. They also freeze well and can be defrosted overnight then reheated in a low oven. **MAKES 12**

2½ cups all-purpose flour

2½ teaspoons baking powder

1½ teaspoons salt

1 teaspoon ground cumin

1 tablespoon granulated sugar

½ cup butter, chilled and cut into cubes

½ cup grated Cheddar cheese

2 tablespoons finely chopped chives

3 large eggs

1 tablespoon water

1. Preheat the oven to 375°F. Line a large baking tray with parchment paper.

2. In a large bowl, sift together the flour, baking powder, salt, and ground cumin. Add the sugar and mix to combine.

3. Add the butter cubes and, using your fingers, quickly rub the butter into the flour mixture until it forms small crumbs. Add the cheese and chives, stirring through.

4. In a small bowl, whisk together the cream and eggs. Gradually add the dry mix, using a fork to help bring it together. It should be soft and slightly sticky. If needed, sprinkle in a little extra flour. Form the mixture into a ball and allow to rest for 5 mintues.

5. On a lightly floured surface, roll the dough out to ¾ inch thick. Using a 1½- to 2-inch fluted cutter, stamp out scones and place them on the lined tray.

6. Lightly brush the scones with an egg wash made from the remaining egg beaten with water. Bake for 12 to 14 minutes, or until puffed and golden brown. Allow to cool slightly before serving.

puddings

BANOFFEE PIE

Though banoffee pie is a classic English dessert made with caramelized condensed milk and bananas, the pecans and graham crackers make it *taste* American. In my version I also include espresso powder for a hint of coffee. It is creamy and delicious and *fun,* and when I serve it at dinner parties, guests almost always go back for more. Rumour has it that banoffee pie was Margaret Thatcher's favourite pudding—it is mine, too. **MAKES 4 TARTS, SERVES 8**

Biscuit Base
1½ cups digestive biscuits or graham crackers (around 8 to 10)
½ cup pecans
½ cup butter, melted

Coffee Caramel
½ cup butter
½ cup brown sugar
1 can (14 ounces) condensed milk
1 teaspoon instant espresso coffee
Pinch of sea salt

Brittle
4 tablespoons granulated sugar
½ cup pecans
1 cup whipping cream
1 tablespoon icing sugar
4 bananas, sliced into rounds
1 tablespoon cocoa powder

1. *To make the biscuit base:* Place the biscuits and pecans in a food processor and pulse until a crumb has formed. Add the melted butter and pulse again until the mixture begins to come together. Press the mixture into four 5-inch fluted tart tins, slightly pushing the mixture up the sides so a small lip forms. Place in the fridge to chill while you prepare the rest.

2. *To make the coffee caramel:* In a medium saucepan over medium heat, add the butter and brown sugar and stir, cooking until dissolved, about 4 minutes. Pour in the condensed milk and bring to a boil. Cook until a thick golden caramel begins to form, stirring constantly until smooth. Remove from the heat and stir through the instant espresso and sea salt. Allow to cool.

3. *For the brittle:* In a small saucepan over medium heat, add the granulated sugar, swirling the pan as it begins to melt. When it has turned a dark amber colour, remove from the heat and stir through the pecans. Tip onto a greased piece of parchment paper to cool completely before roughly cracking.

4. Meanwhile, whisk the cream and icing sugar together until a medium peak has formed.

5. To assemble the pies, line the bases with banana slices in concentric circles. Pour the caramel over the bananas and spread it evenly. Add the remaining bananas, again in a concentric circle. Top with peaks of the whipped cream and candied pecans. Dust with cocoa powder. Chill until ready to serve.

CLASSIC APPLE PIE

When I was a little girl, I would spend summer afternoons at my godmother Kim's house (or rather, my fairy godmother Kim, as I would call her). The most exciting days were those when we made an apple pie together. She would do most of the baking, but I was always given a small ball of pastry to knead and flatten out. I would sprinkle the pastry with cinnamon and sugar and then cut it into little triangles as my own contribution. We would serve my parents slices of the pie with scoops of vanilla ice cream on the side and my cinnamon sugar triangles on top. Now my children do the same, and they stay occupied making their pastry triangles while I bake our apple pie. **SERVES 8 TO 10**

Pastry

1⅔ cups all-purpose flour, plus more for dusting

1 tablespoon sugar

½ teaspoon salt

1 cup cold unsalted butter, cut into cubes

¼ cup ice water

1. *To make the pastry:* In a large bowl, combine the flour, sugar, and salt. Add the butter and quickly rub it into the flour with your fingers until large crumbs form. Add the ice water gradually until the dough begins to come together. Tip onto a clean surface and knead gently until the dough forms. You want to have small pieces of butter visible, as that's what creates the flakiness. Divide the dough in half and refrigerate for at least 30 minutes.

2. *To make the filling:* Combine the apples, raisins, granulated sugar, flour, vanilla bean seeds, salt, and cinnamon in a large bowl. Set aside while you roll out the pastry.

3. On a lightly floured surface, roll out half of the pastry until it is 14 inches in diameter. Gently lift it into a 9-inch pie dish, pressing lightly against the sides and allowing for the pastry to hang over the edge. Using a sharp knife, trim the excess pastry. Place in the fridge to chill while you prepare the lattice.

Filling

**4 to 5 apples, peeled
and cored, then cut
into large pieces**

½ cup raisins

¼ cup granulated sugar

¼ cup flour

**1 vanilla bean, split
and seeds scraped**

¼ teaspoon salt

**2 teaspoons ground
cinnamon**

**1 medium egg, lightly
beaten for egg wash**

**2 tablespoons demerara
sugar**

4. On a lightly floured surface, roll out the other pastry half into a 15-inch x 9-inch rectangle and transfer it to a parchment-lined baking sheet. Wrap both in plastic, and refrigerate for at least 2 hours or overnight.

5. Remove the chilled pie shell from the fridge and fill with the filling. Cut the rectangular pastry into ten 1-inch strips. Place 3 to 5 strips of pastry evenly over the top with about ½-inch spaces between. Fold every other piece back in half. Place a strip down perpendicular to the first strips, unfolding the strips on top. Take the even strips and fold them back. Place another strip of pastry perpendicular and bring the folded ones on top. Repeat until you've formed a lattice. Press the strips into the excess pastry on the edge and trim all the way around. Using your thumb and forefinger, bring the edge up and pinch it to make a nice curvy edge. Chill the pie for at least 30 minutes.

6. Preheat the oven to 400°F, and place the rack in the middle of the oven. Brush egg wash evenly over the pie and sprinkle with demerara sugar. Place on a rimmed baking tray and bake for 40 minutes. Reduce the heat to 180°F and continue to bake for another 20 minutes, or until golden brown, tenting with foil if it's browning too quickly. Remove and allow to cool for at least 15 minutes before serving. Serve with vanilla ice cream.

SOURDOUGH BREAD-AND-BUTTER PUDDING, SERVED WITH A SALTED CARAMEL SAUCE

My great-grandmother was famous in our family for her bread-and-butter pudding. The week's leftover bread was used to make the dessert, as stale bread soaks up butter and cream much better than fresh bread. She always served her bread-and-butter pudding in a bowl and added a bit of cold milk at the end. Now, when my father comes to visit us in London, he asks for his bread-and-butter pudding to be served the same way.

A few years ago, the leftover bread I had on hand was sourdough, so I made my pudding with a loaf of San Francisco sourdough, and the result was a surprising tartness mixed with the sweetness. Since then, I haven't used anything else. **SERVES 6 TO 8**

1 loaf day-old sourdough (I like to leave the crust on, but you can remove it if you want a softer texture to your pudding)

2 tablespoons unsalted butter

½ cup raisins

3 peaches, stones removed, sliced

1 cup plus 3 tablespoons whole milk

⅔ cup light cream

⅔ cup heavy cream

4 large eggs

½ cup coconut sugar

2 large vanilla beans, split and seeds scraped

1 tablespoon ground cinnamon

1. Slather the bread (on both sides!) with the butter—the more generous you are, the better it will taste. Slice the sourdough into roughly ¼-inch-thick pieces and fill your baking dish of choice (a wide, low dish usually works best). Keep in mind that the bread shrinks once the custard mixture is added, so it is okay if the sourdough pieces overfill the dish.

2. Scatter a handful of raisins evenly across the base. Arrange some of the peach slices across the base.

3. Arrange the next base bread layer over the layer of raisins and peaches, followed by a layer of peach wedges—and continue this until you have used all of the bread, raisins, and peaches.

4. Whisk together the milk, cream, eggs, sugar, vanilla seeds, and cinnamon. Pour the mixture over the stale bread. Gently press down with your hand so the bread absorbs the liquid. Let sit for an hour.

5. Preheat the oven to 350°F. Once the bread is drenched and ready, scatter a final layer of peaches on top of the bread and sprinkle with raisins. Place in the oven for 35 minutes.

Salted Caramel Sauce

1 cup sugar
6 tablespoons heavy
    cream
1 tablespoon butter,
    softened
Pinch of sea salt

6. *To make the Salted Caramel Sauce:* In a large saucepan over medium heat, heat the sugar. Gently swirl the pan as the sugar begins to melt, but do not stir. Once the sugar has turned a dark amber, remove it from the heat and carefully pour in the cream. Using a whisk, begin to stir the caramel while adding the softened butter until everything is mixed together. Sprinkle in the salt and whisk well. Pour into a serving container until ready to serve with the pudding.

ETON MESS WITH STRAWBERRY MERINGUES

There are several stories as to why and where Eton mess originated. My favourite is that at the annual cricket match between Eton College and Harrow School, some friends made a beautiful meringue but dropped it after too many Pimm's Cups (see recipe on page 168) and were forced to salvage their meringue mess by adding berries and whipped cream. It is a sweet and playful dessert, very much in the spirit of the origin story. **SERVES 6 TO 8**

Meringues

3 large egg whites, at room temperature

1 cup granulated sugar

⅛ teaspoon cream of tartar

1 tablespoon strawberry jam

4 drops red food coloring

1. *To make the meringues:* Preheat the oven to 225°F. Line 2 baking trays with parchment paper. Place the egg whites into the bowl of a stand mixer and whisk on medium speed until soft peaks begin to form, about 2 minutes. Gradually add the granulated sugar, 1 tablespoon at a time, and the cream of tartar. Whisk until the mixture has stiff peaks and is glossy and smooth, about 5 minutes.

2. Place the strawberry jam and food coloring in a large bowl and stir through one-quarter of the meringue mixture. Fold the pink meringue through the remaining meringue.

3. Using 2 tablespoons, place six to eight ½-cup scoops of meringue onto the parchment paper, swirling it around with the spatula until you have a peaked meringue. They will expand during baking, so make sure to leave space between them. Bake for 2 hours, or until the meringues are dry and crisp. Turn off the oven and leave the meringues to cool in the oven.

recipe continues

Eton Mess

1 cup whipping cream

1 cup plain Greek yoghurt

1 vanilla bean, split and seeds scraped

1 teaspoon rose water

¼ cup icing sugar, sifted

2 cups strawberries

2 tablespoons freeze-dried strawberries (optional)

1 tablespoon rose petals (optional)

2 tablespoons mint leaves

4. *Meanwhile, to make the Eton mess:* In a large bowl, whisk the cream until thickened. In a separate bowl, whisk the yoghurt until smooth then fold through the whipped cream, vanilla bean seeds, rose water, and icing sugar.

5. Roughly chop the strawberries, reserving a few for garnish.

6. To assemble, roughly break up pieces of the meringues. Begin by layering the cream, berries, and meringue in bowls or glasses. Repeat the layering, then garnish with strawberries, freeze-dried berries (if using), rose petals (if using), and mint.

TIPS: *The key to a good meringue is a crisp outer layer and a soft and chewy interior. Be careful not to overwhisk the mixture. You will know you've gone too far if the egg whites look slightly curdled.*

The meringues can be made up to a week in advance and stored in an airtight container.

EVERYTHING COOKIES

Whenever I'm pregnant, I have an impossible time making decisions. The smallest choice can stump me. Give me a menu and I'll stare at it for hours. So over 5 years and three pregnancies, I developed the recipe for these wonderful cookies. There are no decisions to be made—you can have it all! They are also great for kids to make; my own munchkins think it is hilarious to have a cookie with *everything* in it. I like to freeze the unbaked cookies individually so I can bake a couple when I have a craving (which is all of the time, pregnant or not). **MAKES 25 TO 30**

3 cups old-fashioned oats

1 teaspoon ground cinnamon

1 cup all-purpose flour

1 teaspoon baking soda

Pinch of sea salt

1 cup butter, softened

¼ cup natural peanut butter

1 cup brown sugar

¾ cup granulated sugar

2 eggs, at room temperature

1 teaspoon vanilla extract

1½ cups raisins

½ cup chopped walnuts

1 cup semisweet chocolate chips

1. In a bowl, combine the oats, cinnamon, flour, baking soda, and salt.

2. Using an electric mixer, beat together the butter, peanut butter, and sugars until light and fluffy, about 5 minutes. Gradually add the eggs and vanilla, mixing until combined.

3. With the mixer on low speed, add the dry ingredients and mix just to combine.

4. Fold in the raisins, walnuts, and chocolate chips, then chill the mix in the refrigerator for at least 1 hour.

5. Preheat the oven to 350°F. Line 2 baking trays with parchment paper.

6. Take tablespoon amounts of dough and roll them into balls. Place about 1½ inches apart on the baking trays. Bake for 10 to 12 minutes, or until golden. Cool completely on a wire rack.

TIPS: *The most important step that many people overlook when baking cookies is to chill the dough before you bake them, ideally overnight, but if you're short on time, 1 hour will do.*

I use a melon scoop to form the dough balls for consistency in size.

RHUBARB AND APPLE HAZELNUT CRUMBLE

You can use any combination of seasonal fruit for this filling as long as you keep the quantities roughly the same. My grandmother used to make this and serve it warm for breakfast, with cold milk over the top. It makes the most decadent cereal I've ever tasted (and one that I've copied on a few occasions myself when we have some leftovers). **SERVES 6 TO 8**

Topping
⅓ **cup all-purpose flour**
¼ **cup light brown sugar**
½ **teaspoon salt**
1 **cup large flaked oats**
1 **teaspoon ground cinnamon**
½ **teaspoon ground nutmeg**
½ **cup chilled unsalted butter, cut into pieces**
¼ **cup toasted hazelnuts, roughly chopped**

Filling
8–10 **apples, peeled and roughly chopped**
4 to 5 **stalks rhubarb, cut into ¾-inch pieces**
1 **cup granulated sugar**
2 **tablespoons cornstarch**
1 **tablespoon freshly grated orange zest**
2 **tablespoons fresh orange juice**

1. *To make the topping:* In a food processor, combine the flour, sugar, salt, ½ cup of the oats, cinnamon, and nutmeg and pulse in the butter until the mixture is combined. Tip into a bowl and add the remaining ½ cup oats and hazelnuts. Place in the fridge until ready to use.

2. Preheat the oven to 375°F.

3. *To make the filling:* In a large bowl, combine the apples, rhubarb, granulated sugar, cornstarch, orange zest, and orange juice, mixing well to combine. Tip into a 10-inch to 12-inch baking dish and crumble over the topping. Bake for 50 to 60 minutes, or until golden and the fruit is soft. Allow to cool for 30 minutes before serving with vanilla ice cream.

STICKY TOFFEE PUDDING

The sticky toffee pudding at our Bumpkin restaurants is one of our signature British dishes—a real girdle-buster but an unbelievable treat. This pudding is great for dinner parties because it can be made in advance and reheated before serving. The pudding is traditionally baked with the caramel, but I like to make a beautiful Bundt cake and then cover it in salted caramel sauce before serving. **SERVES 6 TO 8**

Cake
2 cups Medjool dates, pitted and roughly chopped
1 teaspoon baking soda
¾ cup butter, softened, plus more for greasing
1 cup brown muscovado sugar
3 large eggs
2 cups all-purpose flour, plus more for dusting
2 teaspoons baking powder
1 teaspoon ground ginger
1 teaspoon ground cinnamon
Pinch of salt

Caramel Sauce
½ cup butter
1 cup brown muscovado sugar
1 cup heavy cream
1 teaspoon sea salt

1. *To make the cake:* Preheat the oven to 350°F. Grease a 9-inch Bundt pan and lightly flour, tapping out the excess. Place the dates and baking soda into a heatproof bowl and cover with 1 cup of just-boiled water. Allow to soak for 15 to 20 minutes, then mash together with a fork.

2. Using an electric mixer, beat the butter and sugar until light and fluffy, about 5 minutes. Gradually add the eggs, beating after each addition, until combined. Then, alternating with the date mixture, add the flour, baking powder, ginger, cinnamon, and salt, beating until combined. Careful not to overmix. Tip the mixture into the prepared pan and bake for 30 to 40 minutes, or until the cake springs back when touched and a skewer inserted in the centre of the cake comes out clean.

3. *To prepare the sauce:* In a pan over medium heat, melt the butter, then add the sugar and cream. Lower the heat and cook, stirring occasionally, until the sauce is golden and thick and coats the back of a spoon. Sprinkle in the salt and remove from the heat.

4. Using a skewer, poke holes into the cooled cake. Drizzle half the sauce over the cake, allowing it to soak in for 15 to 20 minutes. Remove the cake from the pan and drizzle the remaining sauce on top. Slice and serve with a dollop of whipped cream.

CARROT CAKE

Carrot cake is my father's favourite cake, so it always reminds me of summer, when we celebrate his birthday and Father's Day. I also grew up thinking it was healthy—with "carrot" in the title, it had to be, right? This is an undeniably decadent cake, but one to enjoy! **SERVES 8 TO 10**

Cake

½ cup sultanas or raisins

2 tablespoons dark rum

4 eggs

1 cup light brown sugar

1 cup granulated sugar

1 cup butter, melted

1 teaspoon vanilla extract

2½ cups all-purpose flour

2 teaspoons baking powder

1 teaspoon baking soda

1 teaspoon ground cinnamon

1 teaspoon ground ginger

½ teaspoon ground cardamom

1 pound carrots, peeled and grated

1 cup pecans, toasted and roughly chopped (or walnuts, if you prefer)

½ cup buttermilk, at room temperature

1. *To make the cake:* Preheat the oven to 350°F. Grease and line two 8-inch cake pans with parchment paper on the bottoms and sides. Grease and lightly flour the bottoms and sides again, tapping out the excess flour.

2. In a small pan, combine the sultanas or raisins and rum and place over a low heat. Bring to a boil, then remove and allow to cool completely as the sultanas or raisins soak up the liquid.

3. Using an electric mixer, beat the eggs and sugars together until light and thickened, about 1 minute. Gradually add the butter, and continue to whisk until light and fluffy, about 3 minutes. Add the vanilla and combine.

4. In a bowl, whisk together the flour, baking powder, baking soda, cinnamon, ginger, and cardamom. Add the flour mixture to the butter mix, folding together until combined. Fold through the carrots, toasted pecans, and sultanas or raisins, alternately adding buttermilk. Divide the mix between the 2 cake pans and bake for 35 to 45 minutes, or until a skewer comes out clean. Allow to cool for 10 minutes before turning out onto a wire rack to cool completely, about 2 hours.

5. *Meanwhile, to make the brittle:* Line a baking tray with parchment paper and rub the oil all over the paper. Place the pecans on a second baking tray and

recipe continues

Pecan Brittle
1 tablespoon sunflower oil
1 cup pecans
1 cup granulated sugar

Frosting
¾ cup butter, at room temperature
12 ounces cream cheese, at room temperature
4 cups icing sugar
1 teaspoon vanilla extract

pop into the oven for 10 minutes to toast lightly. Place the sugar in a wide saucepan over medium heat and melt it, swirling the pan to get all the bits and pieces. When it begins to turn a nice amber colour, remove from the heat and add the pecans. Swirl them around to coat them in caramel, then pour into a layer on the greased parchment. Allow to cool before placing into a food processor and blitzing until a crumb is formed.

6. *To make the frosting:* With an electric mixer, beat the butter and cream cheese until light and fluffy. Gradually add the icing sugar and vanilla until smooth and creamy.

7. When the cakes are cool, using a serrated knife, carefully and evenly slice them in half horizontally so you have 4 layers.

8. Begin with the domed half of 1 cake and place it upside down. Evenly spread ¼ cup of icing onto the cake. Place the *bottom* layer of that cake on top. Spread another ¼ cup of icing on top and repeat with the other 2 layers.

9. With ½ cup of icing, cover the entire cake. It's okay at this stage for it to be spotty and thin. The idea is to mask the crumbs so the final layer of icing can go on smooth. Place the cake in the fridge for 30 minutes.

10. Evenly spread the remaining icing onto the cake. Sprinkle the pecan brittle on top of the cake.

TIP: *The icing can be made up to 2 weeks in advance and stored in the refrigerator. Allow it to come to room temperature before using.*

GLUTEN-FREE SALTED CARAMEL BROWNIES

I'm not afraid of cooking with real sugar, cream, flour, or chocolate. I buy the highest-quality ingredients that I can find and keep to the mantra of "everything in moderation." That said, one of my best friends is gluten-free, so I devised this recipe for her birthday. I enjoyed it so much that it has become a baking staple in our house.

MAKES 16

Salted Caramel
⅔ **cup granulated sugar**
⅓ **cup heavy cream**
3 **tablespoons butter, cut into pieces and softened**
Pinch of sea salt

Brownies
10 **ounces dark chocolate (75% or higher, roughly chopped)**
6 **ounces milk chocolate**
¾ **cup unsalted butter**
1 **cup granulated sugar**
4 **large eggs, at room temperature**
1 **teaspoon vanilla extract**
½ **cup ground almonds**
½ **cup cocoa powder**
1 **teaspoon instant espresso powder**
1 **teaspoon baking soda**
Pinch of salt

1. *To make the caramel:* In a large saucepan, heat the sugar, swirling the pan as it begins to melt. Once it's turned an amber colour, remove from the heat and carefully pour in the cream, swirling the pan gently. Add the butter in pieces, swirling continuously until everything has melted. Sprinkle in the salt and pour into a bowl to cool.

2. *To make the brownies:* Preheat the oven to 350°F. Grease and line an 8-inch square baking pan with parchment paper.

3. Place the chocolates and butter in a heatproof bowl. Place this on top of a pan of simmering water and melt, stirring occasionally. Carefully remove the bowl from the heat and stir in the sugar, whisking until dissolved. Allow the mix to cool slightly, then gradually whisk in the eggs, one by one, until well incorporated. Add the vanilla, then fold through the ground almonds, cocoa powder, espresso, baking soda, and salt.

4. Pour two-thirds of the brownie batter into the lined pan, spreading it evenly. Add half the caramel and, using the back of a knife, swirl the caramel into the brownie mix. Pour the remaining batter on top and bake for 45 minutes, or until just firm to the touch. Check after 30 minutes, and if the top is starting to look too brown, cover with a piece of foil. Remove from the oven and allow to cool completely in the pan. Gently heat the remaining caramel and drizzle on top before cutting.

CLASSIC LEMON TART

Be sure to allow the pastry to chill and rest before and after you roll it out to ensure it doesn't shrink in the tart pan, as the resting allows the gluten to relax. **SERVES 10**

Pastry

1½ cups all-purpose flour, plus extra for dusting

¾ cup icing sugar, sifted

½ cup cold butter, cut into cubes

3 egg yolks, at room temperature

1 tablespoon lemon zest

½ teaspoon vanilla extract

Filling

5 eggs, at room temperature

¾ cup granulated sugar

⅓ cup plus 1 tablespoon lemon juice (3 lemons)

2 tablespoons lemon zest

⅔ cup heavy cream

Icing sugar, for dusting
Crème fraîche, for serving

1. *To make the pastry:* In a large bowl, combine the flour and sugar, using your fingers to rub the butter into the flour mixture until small crumbs form. Add 2 egg yolks, lemon zest, and vanilla, bringing the dough together into a ball with your fingers. Once the ball is formed, wrap it in plastic wrap and refrigerate it for at least 2 hours.

2. On a lightly floured surface, roll out the pastry, then gently press it into the tart pan. Prick all over with a fork. Refrigerate the shell for at least 1 hour, although overnight is best.

3. Preheat the oven to 375°F. Line the tart shell with parchment paper and pie weights, extending the paper over the pan edges. Bake in the oven for 15 minutes, until the parchment can be lifted without the pastry sticking to it. Carefully remove the weights and paper, and bake the shell for 10 minutes, until golden and crisp.

4. Brush the tart base with the remaining egg yolk and return it to the oven for 1 minute.

5. *To make the filling:* While the base is cooking, whisk together the eggs and sugar until thoroughly combined, about 3 minutes. Add the lemon juice, zest, and heavy cream, whisking until smooth. Set aside.

6. Reduce the oven temperature to 300°F, and carefully pour the lemon filling into the tart shell. Bake for 25 to 30 minutes, until the filling is almost completely set. Remove the tart from the oven and allow it to cool completely, about 2 hours.

7. Dust the tart with icing sugar before serving with crème fraîche.

basics

CASHEW CREAM

Cashew cream is a great vegan and dairy-free alternative to cream. A high-powered blender or food processor is required to get the perfect silky-smooth consistency. This basic recipe can easily be tweaked for sweet and savoury dishes (see one option below using cardamom). **MAKES 1½ CUPS**

1 cup cashews, soaked in cold water for at least 4 hours
Zest of ½ lime
½ cup water
1 teaspoon salt

Drain and rinse the cashews well. Combine the cashews, lime zest, water, and salt in a high-powered blender or a food processor. Blend or process for 2 minutes, or until smooth. Store in an airtight container in the refrigerator for up to 4 days.

CARDAMOM CASHEW CREAM

Great with pancakes! Add these ingredients to the blender along with the ingredients for the basic recipe.

Seeds scraped from 1 vanilla bean
¼ teaspoon ground cardamom
¾ teaspoon ground cinnamon
1 tablespoon maple syrup
Pinch of nutmeg

CLASSIC TOMATO SAUCE

A simple yet classic tomato sauce recipe is one of the best things you can have in your cooking repertoire. This is one of the easiest recipes as everything goes into the blender or food processor and then you cook it over the stove—no fuss of sautéing vegetables, and you end up with a delicious, rich, and well-balanced sauce. **MAKES 3 CUPS**

2 tablespoons olive oil

1 small onion

2 cloves garlic, smashed

2 cans (19 ounces each) San Marzano tomatoes

1 tablespoon brown sugar

Salt and ground black pepper, to taste

1 small handful fresh basil leaves

1. To make the sauce, heat the oil in a large saucepan over medium heat. Add the onion and cook for 10 minutes, or until softened. Add the garlic and cook for another 2 to 3 minutes until fragrant but not brown.

2. Tip in the tomatoes, brown sugar, salt, and pepper, and bring to a boil. Reduce the heat and simmer for 25 to 30 minutes, stirring occasionally. The sauce will be thick. Add the basil and simmer for another 5 minutes. Season with extra salt and pepper, if needed.

STOCKS

Stock cubes are always a quick and easy substitute, but there is nothing like making your own stock from scratch. It doesn't require much of a recipe but rather knowing a few tips and tricks to bring the most flavour out of the vegetables or bones you're cooking from.

Any stock requires a few key ingredients: aromatics, vegetables, and time. Stocks can be chilled completely and kept in the refrigerator for up to 5 days or frozen for up to 3 months.

CHICKEN STOCK

I like to roast the bones and meat, which intensifies the flavour. If you're short on time, you can simply boil them for a couple hours; you will end up with a lighter stock great for quick soups. **MAKES 10½ CUPS**

2 pounds mix of chicken wings and bones, or a carcass

1 onion, unpeeled and quartered

2 carrots, peeled and cut in half

2 celery stalks, cut into thirds

2 bay leaves

1 small bunch flat-leaf parsley, stalks included

1 tablespoon black peppercorns

1 tablespoon sea salt

Ground black pepper, to taste

1. Preheat the oven to 400°F. In a roasting pan, combine the chicken pieces, onion, carrots, and celery. Roast for 25 minutes, or until golden.

2. Place the roasted bone mixture into a large stockpot. Cover completely with water. Add the bay leaves, parsley, peppercorns, and sea salt and bring to a boil. Reduce the heat and simmer for 2 hours, skimming off and discarding any scum that comes to the surface.

3. Strain the stock through a fine mesh sieve into a clean bowl and discard the solids. Season to taste with additional sea salt and ground pepper. Allow to cool completely before chilling.

VEGETABLE STOCK

It's important to caramelize the vegetables in order to intensify the flavour of the stock. **MAKES 8½ CUPS**

2 tablespoons olive oil
1 onion, thickly sliced
1 leek, cleaned and roughly chopped
1 large carrot, roughly chopped
1 bulb fennel, roughly chopped
1 quart water
2 cloves garlic, peeled
2 bay leaves
1 small bunch flat-leaf parsley, stalks included
1 tablespoon black peppercorns
1 tablespoon sea salt

1. In a large stockpot over medium heat, heat the olive oil. Add the onion, leek, carrot, and fennel. Cook for 15 minutes, or until golden and caramelized. Add the water, garlic, bay leaf, parsley, peppercorns, and salt.

2. Bring to a boil, reduce the heat, cover, and simmer for 2 hours, or until it becomes a rich golden colour and becomes fragrant.

3. Strain the stock through a fine mesh sieve into a clean bowl and discard the solids. Allow to cool completely before chilling.

FISH STOCK

Surprisingly simple to make, fish stock is one of the fastest stocks to prepare, as well as one of the best ways to use up fish bones. Be careful not to let it boil for too long or the stock will become bitter. It's important to soak the bones and head in cold water for at least 30 minutes before you begin making the stock to remove any impurities.

1 tablespoon vegetable
   oil
1 bulb fennel, roughly
   chopped
1 celery stalk, roughly
   chopped
1 clove garlic, peeled
1 pound bones from
   white fish,
   including head,
   gills removed
½ cup dry white wine
1 small bunch flat-leaf
   parsley, stalks
   included
1 tablespoon fresh
   tarragon leaves
1 bay leaf
1 tablespoon black
   peppercorns
1 tablespoon sea salt

1. In a large stockpot over medium heat, heat the vegetable oil. Add the fennel and celery and cook for 8 minutes, or until soft and translucent; do not let them colour. Add the garlic along with the fish bones, stirring to coat. Add the wine and cook for 2 minutes. Add the parsley, tarragon, bay leaf, peppercorns, and salt. Add just enough water to cover.

2. Bring to a boil, then reduce the heat and simmer for 30 minutes, skimming off and discarding the scum that comes to the surface.

3. Strain the stock through a fine mesh sieve into a clean bowl and discard the solids. Allow to cool completely before chilling.

TIP: *I like to pour some stock into ice cube trays and freeze it. That way, I have stock cubes ready to use.*

PASTRY RECIPES
SHORTCRUST PASTRY

MAKES 1 TART SHELL

1 cup plus 2 tablespoons all-purpose flour, plus extra for dusting

¾ cup icing sugar, sifted

½ cup butter, cold and diced

1 tablespoon lemon zest

½ teaspoon vanilla extract

2 eggs yolks, at room temperature

1 to 2 tablespoons cold water

1. In a large bowl, combine the flour and sugar. Add the butter and rub it into the flour with your fingers until it resembles large crumbs. Add the lemon zest and vanilla. Gradually add 2 egg yolks, one by one. Gradually add the cold water until the mixture begins to come together.

2. Tip onto a clean surface and knead gently until a dough forms; you want to have small pieces of butter visible because that's what creates the flakiness. Wrap them in plastic wrap and place in the fridge to rest for at least 2 hours. Roll out and bake according to pie recipe directions.

FLAKY PIE PASTRY

MAKES 1 PIE SHELL

1⅔ cups all-purpose flour, plus more for dusting

1 tablespoon sugar

½ teaspoon salt

½ pound unsalted butter, cold and cubed

¼ cup cold water

1. In a large bowl, combine the flour, sugar, and salt. Add the butter and rub it into the flour with your fingers until it resembles large crumbs. Add the cold water gradually until the dough begins to form (you may not need all of the water). Tip onto a clean surface and knead gently. You want to have small pieces of butter visible, as that's what creates the flakiness. Wrap in plastic and place in the fridge for at least 1 hour.

2. After you have rolled out the pastry and are ready to bake, refrigerate the pastry for at least 2 hours to firm up, as the rolling and handling will warm it.

TIP: *Use a glass or aluminum pie dish. They are best for conducting the heat, which allows the butter to steam and create the flaky pastry.*

TOMATO CHUTNEY

This chutney is lovely served as a dollop on top of Corn Fritters (page 18), Welsh Rarebit (page 118), or simply on top of a toasted bagel and cream cheese. **SERVES 6 TO 8**

2 red onions, thinly sliced

2 tablespoons brown sugar

4 cups cherry tomatoes

1 red chili pepper, sliced (wear plastic gloves when handling)

1 tablespoon grated fresh ginger

1 clove garlic, minced

1 tablespoon sherry vinegar

Pinch of salt

In a medium saucepan, combine the onions, sugar, tomatoes, pepper, ginger, garlic, and vinegar. Place over low heat. Gently bring to a boil. Reduce the heat and simmer for 1 hour, stirring occasionally, or until the mixture thickens. Season with the salt. Allow to cool completely. Store in an airtight container in the refrigerator for up to 2 weeks.

NUT BUTTERS

Homemade nut butters are much better than the store variety, and once you make one, you will never turn back. I like to add natural sweeteners such as maple syrup or dates, or even warming spices like cinnamon and nutmeg. You will need a good food processor to make these because it takes a couple minutes for the nuts to release their natural oils and puree into a smooth (or crunchy) butter. Store the finished nut butter in a cool, dry place. It's natural for the oil to separate; just stir before using.

For Almond Cinnamon Butter
2 cups almonds
2 teaspoons ground cinnamon
2 tablespoons coconut oil
3 Medjool dates, pitted
Pinch of salt

For Cashew Cardamom Butter
2 cups cashews, ¼ cup reserved and finely chopped
¼ teaspoon ground cardamom
1½ tablespoons coconut oil
Pinch of salt

For Cocoa Hazelnut Butter
1 cup blanched hazelnuts
1 cup almonds
2 tablespoons maple syrup
1 tablespoon raw cacao powder
1 tablespoon coconut oil
Pinch of sea salt

1. Preheat the oven to 300°F. Place the nuts on a baking tray and bake in the oven for 10 minutes, or until golden and toasted. Allow to cool.

2. Place the cooled nuts and all remaining ingredients in a high-powered food processor and blitz until smooth and creamy. It will take at least 5 minutes.

3. Transfer to airtight containers (for the Cashew Cardamom Butter, first stir in the reserved ¼ cup cashews). Store in the refrigerator or a cool, dry place.

PESTO

Homemade pesto is one of the best ways to use up extra or soon-to-be discarded greens, and you're not limited to herbs. Some of my favourite pestos are made from salad greens like arugula or cavolo nero. Try swapping out the traditional pine nuts for cashews or pumpkin seeds to make an equally delicious version. My ultimate pesto combines herbs and salad greens and is great served with pasta, grilled meats, or simply on top of grilled bread. **SERVES 4**

2 cups basil leaves

1 cup arugula leaves

2 tablespoons fresh coriander leaves

½ cup cashews

1 clove garlic, peeled

¼ cup grated Pecorino Romano cheese

Juice from 1 lemon

⅓ cup plus 1 tablespoon olive oil

Salt and ground black pepper, to taste

1. In a food processor, combine the basil, arugula, coriander, and cashews. Pulse until roughly broken. Add the garlic and pulse again until the mixture begins to come together.

2. Add the cheese and lemon juice. With the motor running, drizzle in the olive oil and blend until smooth. Season with salt and pepper.

ESSENTIAL SALAD DRESSINGS

DIJON-MAPLE DRESSING

1 tablespoon Dijon
    mustard

1 tablespoon maple
    syrup

1 small clove garlic,
    minced

2 tablespoons cider
    vinegar

4 tablespoons olive oil

Salt and ground black
    pepper, to taste

In a small bowl, whisk together the mustard, maple syrup, garlic, and vinegar. Gradually add the olive oil, whisking to combine. Season with salt and pepper.

CITRUS DRESSING

Zest and juice of 1 lime

1 shallot, finely
    chopped

1 teaspoon honey

3 tablespoons olive oil

Salt and ground black
    pepper, to taste

In a small bowl, whisk together the lime zest, lime juice, shallot, honey, and olive oil. Season with salt and pepper.

TAMARI-GINGER DRESSING

1 tablespoon tamari

1 teaspoon grated fresh
    ginger

1 tablespoon sesame oil

½ tablespoon mirin

1 teaspoon honey

Juice of 1 lime

Optional: 1 red chili
    pepper, finely
    chopped (seeds
    removed, if desired)

In a small bowl, whisk together the tamari, ginger, sesame oil, mirin, honey, lime juice, and pepper (if using) until well combined.

HERBY LEMON DRESSING

Juice of 1 lemon

1 clove garlic, peeled
and minced

1 tablespoon finely
chopped fresh
parsley

1 tablespoon finely
chopped fresh mint

1 tablespoon finely
chopped fresh basil

4 tablespoons olive oil

Salt and ground black
pepper, to taste

In a small bowl, whisk together the lemon juice, garlic, parsley, mint, basil, and olive oil. Season with salt and pepper.

GREEN GODDESS DRESSING

1 ripe avocado, pitted
and peeled

Juice of 1 lemon

1 clove garlic, peeled

1 teaspoon honey

2 tablespoons torn
basil leaves

1 teaspoon sea salt

2 tablespoons
grapeseed oil

In a food processor, combine the avocado, lemon juice, garlic, honey, basil, and salt. Process until smooth. With the motor running, add the grapeseed oil and process until combined.

SEASONAL COMPOTES

I love using up summertime fruit and preserving the flavour by making compotes. I serve them on morning toast with butter, or with ice cream or yoghurt, or drizzled over morning oatmeal. These compotes can be made up to 3 days in advance and stored in an airtight container in the refrigerator.

STRAWBERRY, RHUBARB, AND BASIL COMPOTE

MAKES 1½ CUPS

2 cups strawberries, hulled and halved

1 cup rhubarb

¼ cup sugar

1 teaspoon black peppercorns

2 tablespoons water

3–4 basil leaves

In a medium saucepan, combine the strawberries, rhubarb, sugar, peppercorns, and water. Place over medium heat and bring to a boil. Reduce the heat and simmer for 15 to 20 minutes, or until the fruit is tender. Add the basil and stir through. Let cool before serving.

APPLE-VANILLA COMPOTE

MAKES 1½ CUPS

5–6 apples, cored and chopped

½ cup sugar

1 vanilla bean, split and seeds scraped

½ cup water

1 tablespoon lemon juice

In a medium saucepan, combine the apples, sugar, vanilla seeds, and water. Place over medium heat and bring to a boil. Reduce the heat and simmer for 20 to 25 minutes, or until the apples are tender. Stir in the lemon juice. Let cool before serving.

PEACH AND CARDAMOM COMPOTE

MAKES 1½ CUPS

**4 peaches, pitted,
    peeled, and roughly
    chopped**
¼ cup sugar
**¼ teaspoon ground
    cardamom**
**¼ teaspoon ground
    cinnamon**
¼ cup water
**1 tablespoon lemon
    juice**

In a medium saucepan, combine the peaches, sugar, cardamom, cinnamon, and water. Place over medium heat and bring to a boil. Reduce the heat and simmer for 15 to 20 minutes, or until the peaches are tender. Stir in the lemon juice. Let cool before serving.

acknowledgments

THE BIGGEST THANKS TO MY HUSBAND, MATT, FOR BELIEVING IN ME AND for peeling me off the ceiling when I was so anxious about everything concerning this book—the writing, the recipe testing, the deadlines. And for taking the kids out to the park on Saturday afternoons so I could hunker down and write or measure flour without distraction. And to our beautiful boys, Max and Jake—thank you for all the stirring and egg cracking help you did for Mummy's book—and to our darling sous-chef, Sadie, who sat in her bouncy chair and cooed at me while I stood at the stove. Thank you all for supporting me through this—and for tasting all of my recipes a thousand and one times.

To my most-patient-editor-on-the-planet, Dervla Kelly, who believed in me from the beginning, patiently waited while I translated from metric to Americana (imperial), and juggled time zones with ease! To Rae Ann Spitzenberger, for making this book look so pretty (wow!) and to the rest of the Rodale Team—Anna Cooperberg, Aly Mostel, Susan Turner, Angie Giammarino, and Hope Clarke—who have all made this book happen. Helen Cathcart, you've taken the prettiest pictures of my family and food; and Linda Berlin, thank you for bringing the loveliest props and especially for making the apron that I'm wearing on the cover!

To my food writers and recipe testers, Dara Sutin and Becci Woods, for all of your time and dedication to this book. To Jo Rodgers, for being my second set of eyes and an even better writer! To Julie Montagu, who I met while filming *Ladies of London,* who is a veteran in the cookbook industry, and who kept supporting me through this adventure. To Teal, without you, this book might never have happened—you pushed it along and got it done! To Eve Atterman at WME, thank you for believing in me from the beginning and for finding this book a home.

And to everyone who has supported me through this and tasted all of my recipes along the way—or as Max has said, "I've tasted your lasagne infinity and one times, Mummy. It is GOOD!"

index

Boldface page references indicate photographs.